Philosophy of Religion: A Very Short Introduction

VERY SHORT INTRODUCTIONS are for anyone wanting a stimulating and accessible way into a new subject. They are written by experts, and have been translated into more than 45 different languages.

The series began in 1995, and now covers a wide variety of topics in every discipline. The VSI library currently contains over 550 volumes—a Very Short Introduction to everything from Psychology and Philosophy of Science to American History and Relativity—and continues to grow in every subject area.

Very Short Introductions available now:

ACCOUNTING Christopher Nobes
ADOLESCENCE Peter K. Smith
ADVERTISING Winston Fletcher
AFRICAN AMERICAN RELIGION
    Eddie S. Glaude Jr
AFRICAN HISTORY John Parker and
    Richard Rathbone
AFRICAN RELIGIONS
    Jacob K. Olupona
AGEING Nancy A. Pachana
AGNOSTICISM Robin Le Poidevin
AGRICULTURE Paul Brassley and
    Richard Soffe
ALEXANDER THE GREAT
    Hugh Bowden
ALGEBRA Peter M. Higgins
AMERICAN HISTORY Paul S. Boyer
AMERICAN IMMIGRATION
    David A. Gerber
AMERICAN LEGAL HISTORY
    G. Edward White
AMERICAN POLITICAL HISTORY
    Donald Critchlow
AMERICAN POLITICAL PARTIES
    AND ELECTIONS L. Sandy Maisel
AMERICAN POLITICS
    Richard M. Valelly
THE AMERICAN PRESIDENCY
    Charles O. Jones
THE AMERICAN REVOLUTION
    Robert J. Allison
AMERICAN SLAVERY
    Heather Andrea Williams
THE AMERICAN WEST Stephen Aron

AMERICAN WOMEN'S HISTORY
    Susan Ware
ANAESTHESIA Aidan O'Donnell
ANALYTIC PHILOSOPHY
    Michael Beaney
ANARCHISM Colin Ward
ANCIENT ASSYRIA Karen Radner
ANCIENT EGYPT Ian Shaw
ANCIENT EGYPTIAN ART AND
    ARCHITECTURE Christina Riggs
ANCIENT GREECE Paul Cartledge
THE ANCIENT NEAR EAST
    Amanda H. Podany
ANCIENT PHILOSOPHY Julia Annas
ANCIENT WARFARE
    Harry Sidebottom
ANGELS David Albert Jones
ANGLICANISM Mark Chapman
THE ANGLO-SAXON AGE John Blair
ANIMAL BEHAVIOUR
    Tristram D. Wyatt
THE ANIMAL KINGDOM
    Peter Holland
ANIMAL RIGHTS David DeGrazia
THE ANTARCTIC Klaus Dodds
ANTISEMITISM Steven Beller
ANXIETY Daniel Freeman and
    Jason Freeman
THE APOCRYPHAL GOSPELS
    Paul Foster
ARCHAEOLOGY Paul Bahn
ARCHITECTURE Andrew Ballantyne
ARISTOCRACY William Doyle
ARISTOTLE Jonathan Barnes

Available soon:

For more information visit our website

www.oup.com/vsi/

Tim Bayne

PHILOSOPHY
OF RELIGION

A Very Short Introduction

OXFORD
UNIVERSITY PRESS

OXFORD
UNIVERSITY PRESS

Great Clarendon Street, Oxford, OX2 6DP,
United Kingdom

Oxford University Press is a department of the University of Oxford.
It furthers the University's objective of excellence in research, scholarship,
and education by publishing worldwide. Oxford is a registered trade mark of
Oxford University Press in the UK and in certain other countries

Published in the United States of America by Oxford University Press
198 Madison Avenue, New York, NY 10016, United States of America

British Library Cataloguing in Publication Data
Data available

Library of Congress Control Number: 2017955187

ISBN 978-0-19-875496-1

Printed and bound by CPI Group (UK) Ltd, Croydon, CR0 4YY

For Keith Howard and Malcolm Millar

Contents

List of illustrations

Note on language

I have avoided the use of gender-specific pronouns in this volume, replacing 'God himself' with 'God Godself'. Although English traditionally associates God with masculine pronouns, readers might be interested to discover that in other languages terms for the divine are associated with both masculine and feminine genders. For example, the grammatical gender of the 'Spirit' is feminine in Hebrew (רוּחַ, rūaḥ), as is 'shekhinah', a term that is used in rabbinical writings to indicate the presence of God. In Islam, the essence of God is known as *al-Dhat*, a term that is grammatically feminine.

Note on dates

Although dates for Islamic philosophers are typically given in terms of the Hijri era (which began when Muhammad and his followers migrated from Mecca), for ease of comparison across different religious traditions all dates here are given in terms of the Common Era (CE).

Chapter 1
What is the philosophy of religion?

Athens and Jerusalem

The philosophy of religion is concerned not with religion as a
social, cultural, or political phenomenon, but with philosophical
questions that are prompted by religious faith and experience.
Some of these questions concern religion in general. For example,
philosophers of religion are interested in the nature of religious
experience, and whether it provides evidence for the existence of a
supernatural realm. Some of these questions concern particular
families of religions. For example, philosophers of religion are
interested in the conception of God that is endorsed by adherents
of the Abrahamic faiths (that is, Judaism, Christianity, and Islam),
and whether there are good reasons to think that God as conceived
of by these faiths exists. And some of these questions concern
particular religious traditions. For example, philosophers of religion
consider whether the Christian doctrine of the Trinity—the claim
that God is 'three persons in one'—is intelligible, or whether
the Buddhist rejection of the self is consistent with the theory
of karma.

The foregoing might suggest that there is a close connection
between the philosophy of religion and theology. After all, isn't
theology also concerned with questions pertaining to the existence
of God, the nature of religious belief, and the like? There is indeed

1

an intimate relationship between these two disciplines, and the nature and location of the border between them is a matter of some dispute. One approach to distinguishing theology from the philosophy of religion appeals to the perspective that one adopts in attempting to answer a particular question. Theological discussions occur *within* the context of a particular religious tradition, whereas philosophical discussions aim to *transcend* the boundaries between traditions. Suppose that you are considering whether God could have created time. In the context of a theological discussion it might be appropriate to appeal to the authority of a religious text or scholar in answering this issue, but such appeals won't typically be appropriate if one is engaged in the philosophy of religion, for the religious authorities that are recognized by the members of one religious tradition are unlikely to be recognized by the members of other religious traditions. This does not mean that the philosophy of religion is restricted only to those who do not identify with a particular religion, but it does mean that the kinds of considerations that one can appeal to insofar as one is engaging in the philosophy of religion are considerations that ought, in principle at least, to be compelling to people irrespective of their religious convictions.

Religions exhibit a wide variety of attitudes towards philosophy (and indeed towards philosophers!). Some religions embrace philosophical reflection. In fact, there are a number of religions—Buddhism, Hinduism, and Taoism, for example—in which the very distinction between philosophy and religion is far from clear-cut, and certain strands within these religions are as much philosophical systems as they are religious ones. Other religions display a more ambivalent attitude towards philosophy. This ambivalence is particularly marked with respect to the Abrahamic religions. The scriptures of Judaism, Christianity, and Islam contain very little in the way of explicit philosophical reflection, and the claims that they make concerning God and reality are typically based not on argument but on appeals to revelation and the word of the prophets. Indeed, suspicion of philosophical methods is a common theme in the Abrahamic religions. This suspicion was pithily captured by the 2nd-century Christian theologian Tertullian when he asked: 'What has Athens to do with Jerusalem?' Athens, of course, represented the Greek philosophical tradition, whereas Jerusalem represented the Hebrew prophetic tradition.

However, the relationship between the Abrahamic faiths and philosophical reflection is a complex one. Although many have contrasted 'The God of the philosophers' with 'The God of Abraham, Isaac and Jacob' (as the French philosopher Blaise Pascal put it), the Abrahamic faiths boast long histories of sophisticated philosophical reflection on religious matters. Christian philosophers who have made important contributions to the philosophy of religion include St Augustine (354–430), St Thomas Aquinas (1225–74), John Duns Scotus (1266–1308), William of Ockham (1287–1347), René Descartes (1596–1650), John Locke (1632–1704), and Gottfried Wilhelm Leibniz (1646–1716). Jewish philosophers who have made important contributions to the philosophy of religion include Maimonides (1135–1204), Gersonides (1288–1344), and Spinoza (1632–77). And among the many Islamic thinkers who have made major contribution to the philosophy of religion are Al-Kindi (*c*.800–870), Al-Farabi (*c*.870–*c*.950), Al-Ghazali (*c*.1056–1111), Ibn Rushd (1126–98; also known as Averroes), and Ibn Sina (*c*.970–1037; also known as Avicenna). Although these thinkers belong to very different social contexts and religious traditions, they all take philosophy to have a central role to play when it comes to religious matters.

Just a matter of opinion?

Despite the long history of philosophical reflection on religious issues, many people are surprised to discover that there is such an enterprise as the philosophy of religion. Religion and philosophy, they assume, are like oil and water: they just don't mix. What might motivate this attitude, and is there any reason to endorse it?

Some hold that philosophy and religion should be kept apart on the grounds that questions about God's existence (for example) are simply beyond the reach of philosophical methods. Religious issues—so this line of thought runs—are matters of taste and opinion rather than reason and argument. One might choose to believe that God exists—or, as the case may be, that God doesn't exist—but such questions can't be settled by reason and even considering the relevant arguments is a waste of time.

Although the position just expressed is not uncommon, there is little to recommend it. For one thing, it is far from obvious that questions about God's existence *are* beyond the reach of human reason. A great many thinkers down the ages—not to mention a great many contemporary thinkers—would certainly reject that assertion. To demonstrate that religious issues are beyond the reach of human reason one would first need to provide an account of the limits of human reason, and then show that religious matters lie beyond those limits. Such an enterprise has occasionally been attempted—the Prussian philosopher Immanuel Kant famously argued for a version of this view—but few theorists regard such attempts as successful. The philosophy of religion may not be able to provide definitive answers to the questions that it asks, but it would not be unreasonable to hope that it can at least illuminate them.

There is certainly no doubt that people *do* appeal to philosophical considerations when discussing religious matters. They consider arguments for and against God's existence; they wonder whether divine omniscience is compatible with free will; and they puzzle over the possibility of miracles or the prospects of life after death. Of course, it can be argued that these considerations have little impact on the religious views that people hold. It is certainly true that the levers of belief are not moved by the force of reason alone; indeed, when it comes to religious matters it's doubtful whether reason is even the primary source of belief. But although philosophical considerations are far from being the only drivers of belief, they can—and often do—have an impact on a person's religious convictions.

A second argument for thinking that religion and philosophy ought to be kept apart concerns issues of autonomy and religious freedom. One might be tempted to argue that if it were legitimate to appeal to philosophical considerations in adjudicating issues of faith, then religious convictions that could be shown to be irrational might be regarded as suspect, and that—one might worry—would in turn be at odds with deeply cherished ideals concerning religious liberty and autonomy.

We can see that there must be something wrong with this argument by observing that there is no inconsistency in holding both that political discussion ought to be informed by philosophical considerations and that freedom of political thought should be respected. Where then does the argument go wrong? It goes wrong in assuming that presenting a person with objections to their views involves infringing their freedom of belief. Although certain ways of altering a person's beliefs—for example, by drugging them or subjecting them to emotional pressure—do undermine a person's autonomy, other methods do not. Crucially, the methods of persuasion employed in philosophy are autonomy-respecting, for philosophical arguments appeal only to considerations that are rationally compelling. Thus, far from undermining an individual's autonomy, philosophical engagement is actually a form of respecting that autonomy. Besides, the primary focus of the philosopher of religion is not with the critical evaluation of anyone else's views but with the critical evaluation of one's own views.

With that thought in mind let's get to work.

Chapter 2
The concept of God

Classical theism

Religions differ widely in their conceptions of God's nature. Some religions conceive of God as a being that brought the world into existence but has since left it to its own devices, whereas others conceive of God as actively engaged with the world of human affairs—answering prayer, performing miracles, and speaking to humanity. Some religions regard God as a unity, whereas others take God to be triune (that is, to be three persons in one being). Some religions take God to have been incarnated in human form, whereas others recoil in horror from any such suggestion. Some religions hold that there is but one God, whereas other religions are polytheistic, positing many gods, each with its own jurisdiction. Some religions conceive of God as a supernatural being—an entity that is distinct from cosmos, whereas others identify God with the totality of all that there is.

Rather than consider each of these various conceptions of God, we will restrict our attention to what philosophers of religion call 'classical monotheism', and we will leave other religious perspectives—such as those found in Buddhism, Taoism, and polytheism, for example—to one side. Classical monotheists distinguish themselves from both henotheists (who hold that there are many gods, one of which is supreme) and pantheists (who identify God with the world). They also distinguish themselves from deists. Theists regard God as personal, and as participating in an on-going relationship with humanity. They take God to have knowledge, to exercise free will, and to enter into relationships with individuals and communities. Indeed, the claim that we are made in the image of God (Genesis 1:27) is often taken by theists to imply that our personhood is a reflection of God's own personhood. Deists, by contrast, conceive of God in rather more impersonal terms—as a cosmic engineer who created the world but has no on-going relationship with it.

We will focus on classical monotheism (hereafter simply 'theism') not because other conceptions of God and ultimate reality are devoid of philosophical interest, but because theism has dominated philosophy of religion within the Western world. Theism lies at the heart of the Abrahamic religions of Judaism, Christianity, and Islam, and it can also be found in certain strands of Hinduism. Many of the most prominent philosophers have themselves been theists; understandably, they have focused their attention on the nature of God as understood within their religious traditions. A further reason for the emphasis on theism within the philosophy of religion is that critics have often charged that the theistic concept of God is incoherent, and that it ascribes to God properties that no being could possibly have. In this sense, they liken the theist's concept of God to the concept of a square circle: neither concept, they claim, could possibly have instances. This charge poses a fundamental challenge to theism, for if it can be sustained then it would follow that the God of theism not only does not exist but *could not* exist. For this reason, many discussion of whether God exists begin with the questions about the analysis of the concept of God.

Perfect Being Theology

How are we to decide what properties to ascribe to the God of theism? This question looks like it ought to have a straightforward answer, for religious traditions are replete with claims about the nature of God. Why can't we simply consult the scriptures of (say) Judaism, Christianity, or Islam in order to determine what properties theism (or, more precisely, a particular variant thereof) ascribes to God?

But although most philosophers of religion would agree that any analysis of the concept of God must be anchored to religious texts in some way, few think that we can simply 'read-off' God's properties from the pages of sacred scriptures. Religious texts are rarely written to address philosophical concerns, and they typically lack the precision required for philosophical analysis. For example, the Gospel of Matthew reports Jesus as saying that nothing is impossible for God, but nowhere does it engage with the question of whether God can make a stone that even God cannot lift.

Philosophers of religion respond to the silence of scripture in various ways. Some argue that our knowledge of God's nature is solely dependent on revelation, and as a result questions about God's nature that are not settled by scripture are questions that cannot be answered. Those who belong to this tradition often emphasize the transcendence of the divine, arguing that God is fundamentally unknowable. Other philosophers of religion hold that reason can provide at least some insight into the nature of God. This approach is known as 'natural theology'—'natural' because it appeals to our natural capacities for reasoning.

One of the most influential traditions within natural theology begins with the idea that God must be perfect in every respect, for an imperfect being would not be worthy of our worship in the way in which God is (and must be). Having established the perfection of God, these theorists then attempt to develop a substantive account of God's nature, arguing that perfection does—or, as the case may be, does not—require the possession of certain properties. For example, they argue that God must be omnipotent (able to do anything), for power is a perfection (a 'good-making property'), and thus a being that failed to be omnipotent would not be perfect. This approach—known as 'Perfect Being Theology'—has its roots in St Augustine and the ancient Greek philosophical tradition, but it is most closely associated with the medieval philosopher St Anselm (1033–1109), whose famous ontological proof for the existence of God begins from the assumption that the concept of God is the concept of a being who possesses all perfections. (The ontological argument attempts to establish the existence of God from the fact that the concept of God is the concept of a being 'than which nothing greater can be conceived'. If God doesn't exist in reality, the argument continues, it would follow that there could be a being that was greater than God, for a being that exists in reality is greater than one which is exists only 'in the understanding'—that is, as a concept.) For this reason Perfect Being Theology is sometimes referred to as 'Anselmian theology'.

Perfect Being Theology has had a profound impact on contemporary philosophy of religion, and there are few discussions of the concept of God that are not influenced by it in some way or another. However, the approach is also open to a number of serious—indeed, in my view, fatal—objections.

Most fundamentally, it is unclear whether the notion of a supremely perfect being is coherent. Talk of 'a perfect x' is certainly intelligible for some instances of x. Although neither a perfect circle nor a perfectly smooth surface can exist in the physical world, these concepts are perfectly intelligible, for we know precisely what it would take for there to be a perfect circle or a perfectly smooth surface. But there are other concepts for which talk of 'a perfect x' is of dubious intelligibility. What would it take to be a perfect book? A perfect vegetable? A perfect jazz solo? Just as it is doubtful whether the notion of perfection has genuine purchase when applied to these domains, so too one might doubt whether the notion has genuine purchase when applied to the category of 'being'. What precisely would it take for a *being* to be perfect?

Advocates of Perfect Being Theology respond to this question by arguing that certain properties—such as power and knowledge—are intrinsically valuable. Possessing these properties, they claim, increases a being's excellence no matter what kind of being it is. Thus, creatures that possess fewer of these properties, or possess these properties to lesser degrees, are less excellent—'less perfect'—than creatures that possess more of these properties or possess them to greater degrees. A maximally perfect being would thus be a being that possessed all 'good-making' properties and did so to the maximal degree possible.

Several aspects of this picture might strike one as unsatisfactory. (They certainly strike *me* as unsatisfactory.) For one thing, the idea that the excellence of a being depends on the degree to which it is powerful or knowledgeable seems odd. After all, we don't typically regard the excellence of human beings as dependent on their power or knowledge. I know more than my 6-year-old nephew does, and I can certainly do more than he can, but surely that does not make me more 'excellent' than he is. Moreover, even if power and knowledge do confer excellence on those who possess them, why suppose that they have any limit? Why not suppose that for every powerful and knowledgeable being, there is—or at least could be—another being that is more powerful and knowledgeable than the first? And if that were the case then the very notion of a perfect being would be incoherent, even if power and knowledge were good-making properties.

Of course, Perfect Being Theologians need not regard power and knowledge as good-making properties (although, for the record, they typically do), but if these properties aren't good-making then what properties are? Perfect Being Theology provides a useful guide to God's nature only if we have the capacity to discern whether having a certain property contributes to a being's excellence, and it is far from clear that we do. Consider the property of simplicity. Some Perfect Being Theologians argue that God must be simple on the grounds that simplicity is a good-making property. But why suppose that simple beings are objectively more excellent than complex ones, rather than vice-versa? Perfect Being Theology presupposes an optimistic conception of our capacity to comprehend the ways of God—a conception that would seem to be at odds with the pessimistic attitude that theists often adopt when faced with the question of why God permits evil (see Chapter 5).

But if we can't appeal to the notion of a perfect being in order to ground our analysis of the concept of God how then are we to proceed? How *should* we go about determining what properties to assign to the God of theism?

I doubt that there is any fully general answer to this question. Instead of embracing a single method for resolving questions about the concept of God (as Perfect Being Theology does), perhaps we have no option but to muddle our way through, critically reflecting on the various attributes that are ascribed to God in the light of commonly endorsed theological and philosophical assumptions. So let us do just that, focusing our attention on three of the central properties that theists assign to God: being the creator of the world, being all-knowing (or 'omniscient'), and being the proper object of our worship.

Creation

The conception of God as the creator lies at the very heart of classical theism. Many readers will be familiar with the opening verses of the book of Genesis, according to which God created 'the heavens and the earth' (see Figure 1). But what precisely does 'the heavens and the earth' include? Does it include time? Does it include abstract entities such as numbers? Does it include the laws of morality? The author of Genesis simply doesn't say.

1. Urizen measuring out the material world from 'The Ancient of Days', by William Blake.

Philosophical reflection on these questions begins with a distinction between two types of facts: contingent facts and necessary facts. Contingent facts are so-called because although they obtain they might not have obtained. The fact that you are reading this book is almost certainly contingent, for there are many other things that you might have done with your time. By contrast, necessary facts are so-called because there is no way that they could not have obtained. Many philosophers have held that mathematical facts are necessary. The sum of one and two doesn't merely happen to be three—rather, there is no way in which it could have been anything other than three.

Theists typically take God's creative activity to encompass all contingent facts, such as those that concern the existence of badgers, ballerinas, and the Brooklyn Bridge. Of course, theists don't (or at least need not) deny that evolutionary forces played a role in the origin of badgers; that distinctive cultural conditions are required for the existence of ballerinas; or that the Brooklyn bridge was built by human engineers. Their claim is only that God's creative activity underpins the existence of badgers, ballerinas, and the Brooklyn Bridge in that God is responsible for the fundamental particles that populate the physical universe and the laws that govern their behaviour, and, without these particles and laws, badgers, ballerinas, and bridges would not be possible. But what about those elements of reality that are necessary, such as mathematical facts? Is God also responsible for these features of reality?

Many theists have thought not. As they see things, the fact that electrons have a negative charge is dependent on God's creative activity, whereas the fact that seven is a prime number is not. But although this is the mainstream view, there are also influential voices of dissent. The philosopher and mathematician René Descartes (1596–1650), for one, held that even mathematical facts depend on God. To regard such facts as independent of God, Descartes claimed, would be to regard God 'as if He were [the Roman gods] Jupiter or Saturn'—that is, as nothing more than some kind of 'superman'. Descartes granted that we cannot conceive of a situation in which the sum of one and two failed to be three, but he regarded this as nothing more than a manifestation of human limitation rather than any kind of insight into a realm of necessity that might constrain God.

Mathematical facts aren't the only kinds of facts that raise tricky questions about the scope of God's creative power. Moral facts do too. Should theists regard morality as independent of God, or should they instead take moral facts to depend on God in the way in which physical facts do? There are objections to both of these positions. On the one hand, theists are typically reluctant to regard moral facts as independent of God's creative power, for they worry that adopting that position would infringe God's sovereignty. On the other hand, theists are reluctant to regard moral facts as dependent on God's creative power, for if the laws of morality depend on God then it is presumably within God's power to alter them, just as it is presumably within God's power to alter the laws of physics. But—so the worry runs—surely the laws of morality can't be altered—even by God.

This challenge is known as Euthyphro's dilemma, for it was first articulated by Plato in his dialogue 'Euthyphro'. Some theists argue that one or other of the two horns of this dilemma is not as sharp as it might seem; others argue that it possible to find a way between them, and that moral facts can depend on God without being contingent. In short, whether morality should be included with the scope of the created order remains a disputed issue.

Having considered certain aspects of the 'what' of creation, let us turn our attention to the 'how' of creation. How might God have created the universe?

In addressing this question, it is natural to begin by reflecting on the construction of material goods, such as cakes, kayaks, and kimonos. However, it doesn't take much thought to realize that the creation of such goods provides a poor model for God's creation of the world. For one thing, we create physical artefacts by modifying matter, whereas theists take God to have created the

14

world from nothing—*ex nihilo*, as the Latin phrase puts it. A second contrast is that the construction of physical artefacts requires moving one's body in some manner, whereas theists typically deny that God has a body. (Some theists regard the world as God's body, but that view is of no help here given that our question is how God might have made the world in the first place.)

There are, however, other models that we might appeal to in attempting to understand divine creation. Human creativity is not limited to the construction of material goods but includes symphonies, mathematical proofs, and fictional worlds. Just as J.R.R. Tolkien brought Middle Earth and its inhabitants into being with an act of imagination, so too—the theist might argue—the actual world was brought into being by an act of the divine imagination. Might the creation of fictional worlds provide a better model for understanding God's creative activity than that which is provided by the construction of physical artefacts?

Perhaps, but theists should be wary of pushing the fictional model too far, for there are important contrasts between fictional worlds and the actual world. Most fundamentally, the actual world is populated by entities that are genuine agents in their own right, whereas that is not true of fictional worlds. Fictional worlds do of course contain agents, but their agency is a degenerate kind of agency. According to Tolkien's narrative, Gandolf has the power to bring things about in Middle Earth, but his powers are utterly parasitic on Tolkien's decisions. (Novelists do sometimes describe their characters as taking on a life of their own, but they are of course speaking figuratively.) By contrast, the theist sees the relationship between God and human agents rather differently. We are not merely characters in God's screenplay, but are independent agents who can both affect and in turn be affected by God's actions. So neither the creation of material goods nor the creation of fictional worlds provides a fully satisfying model for how God might have created the world. Theists still have work to do in providing an account of the 'how' of creation.

A final question regarding God's creative activity concerns God's reason for creating the world. This is the 'why' of creation. Human creation is typically driven by need and desire. We build houses in order to stay warm and dry; we plant crops in order to feed ourselves; and we exercise in order to stay healthy. Did God create the world in order to meet some need or to satisfy some desire? According to one Islamic hadith, when the prophet David asked for the purpose of creation Allah responded, 'I was a hidden treasure and desired to be known.' But the suggestion that God had desires that could be satisfied only by creation has struck many theists as heretical. God—so many theists claim—is complete in Godself; God needs nothing from us. But if creation was not motivated by need what did motivate it?

One of the most interesting responses to this question is to be found in the Hindu tradition. Reflecting on God's motives for creating the world, the authors of the Brahma Sutra (II.1.33) suggest that Brahma (the creator God) fashioned the world through an act of *līlā*, a term that is typically translated as 'play' or 'sport'. In his commentary on this passage the 12th-century philosopher Ramanuja suggested that Brahma's creative activity might be likened to the activity of a king who engages in a game 'for no other reason than to amuse himself'. God's creation of the world was, Ramanuja suggests, purely spontaneous and non-purposive, an act that was not motivated by the attempt to assuage any need or satisfy any desire. I will leave you to consider the merits of this explanation for creation, or indeed of any other explanation that you can think of.

Knowledge

In addition to conceiving of God as a creator, theists also conceive of God as omniscient. There are two sources for this commitment. One is the familiar Anselmian idea that knowledge is a perfection—where that is taken to imply that God must be unsurpassable in knowledge, and that in turn is taken to require that God must be all-knowing. The second reason for thinking that God must be omniscient derives from religious texts, for the scriptures of many monotheistic religions suggest that God is omniscient. For example, the Koran states: 'You have no need to speak aloud; for He has knowledge of all that is secret, and all that is hidden.... God has knowledge of all things.'

The doctrine of omniscience raises two questions. The first concerns its content: what precisely does it mean to say that God is omniscient? The second question concerns the consistency of the claim that God is omniscient with other claims that theists might want to make, such as the claim that human beings have free will. These questions are not unrelated, for the theist who discovers that a certain conception of omniscience is inconsistent with other views that she has might take herself to have a reason to revise that conception of omniscience.

On the most straightforward understanding of omniscience, God is omniscient if and only if it is the case that for every true proposition P God knows that P is true, and for every false proposition P God knows that P is false. Could God be omniscient in this sense?

One reason to think not involves propositions that describe certain aspects of human experience. Could God know what it's like to feel ashamed? To struggle with temptation? To experience frustration, uncertainty, or ignorance? Knowledge of the relevant kind seems to require precisely the kind of limited and flawed perspective that would not be available to God. Ironically, it is precisely God's perfection that threatens to render certain forms of knowledge—that is, knowledge of states that involve imperfection—divinely inaccessible. (Versions of theism—such as Christianity—which take God to have become incarnate in human form may have the resources to respond to this objection, but the doctrine of the incarnation raises philosophical puzzles of its own.)

A second challenge to the idea that God could be omniscient concerns human freedom. Suppose that tomorrow you freely decide to take your dog for a walk. It follows that there is now a true proposition to the effect that you will take your dog for a walk tomorrow. Propositions of this kind are known as future contingents. Thus, if God is omniscient, and if omniscience requires knowledge of all true propositions, then God now knows that tomorrow you will take your dog for a walk. But—so the argument runs—if God now knows that you're going to take your dog for a walk then you cannot do so freely, for if this decision were free then you could refrain from making it, but if you were able to do that then you would be able to make it the case that God has a false belief. However, you aren't able to make it the case that God has a false belief, for that would be at odds with the fact that God is omniscient, and essentially so. This argument generalizes to any future free act—any 'future contingent'—to generate a dilemma for the theist: either God isn't omniscient, or genuinely free action is not possible. Given that few theists are willing to deny the possibility of free agency, the argument threatens to force them to reject God's omniscience.

This is one of the most widely discussed arguments in the philosophy of religion. We cannot consider each of the various responses that have been made to it, but will instead restrict our attention to two of the most interesting.

The first response takes issue with the assumption that there are propositions about future contingents. According to this line of thought, if the future is genuinely open—if, that is, it is now possible for you to take your dog for a walk tomorrow and also possible for you to refrain from taking your dog for a walk—then it is not the case that there is now a true propositions to the effect that tomorrow you will take your dog for a walk. And if there is no such proposition then there is nothing for an omniscient being to know (or indeed fail to know). It is only when you actually take your dog for a walk that the relevant proposition comes into existence.

Evaluating the merits of this argument would require us to explore the nature of propositions, and that is a project for another occasion. What we can say here is that even if this response is philosophically defensible it may not survive theological scrutiny. If future contingents fall outside the scope of God's knowledge, then creation was a massive gamble, for God didn't know what human beings would do with their capacity for free agency. The God of theism, however, is not normally thought of as a dice-player (to echo Einstein's famous comment).

A second response to the challenge from future contingents concerns the assumptions that it makes about God's relationship to time. In presenting the challenge we assumed that God is located in time in the way that we are. In other words, we assumed that some events take place in God's present, others take place in God's past, and still others take place in God's future. Many theists have argued that this view is mistaken, and that God's relationship to time is utterly unlike our own. In the words of the philosopher Boethius (c.475–526 CE), God's eternity consists in the 'complete possession of an endless life enjoyed as one simultaneous whole'.

The view that God exists 'outside' of time is known as atemporalism. According to the atemporalist, God's properties are not indexed to particular times in the way in which our properties are. We have properties at particular times—for example, you have the property of being asleep at some times but not at others—but the atemporalist denies that God has properties at particular times. On this view, God no more has a history or a future than abstract entities such as numbers do. Just as it is incoherent to ask how long the number eight has been in existence or to wonder how long it will continue to exist, so too the atemporalist thinks that such questions are incoherent when asked of God.

How might atemporalism bear on the challenge of future contingents? The idea is as follows. Suppose that you do indeed take your dog for a walk tomorrow. This event occurs in the future relative to your current temporal perspective, but it is not—nor was it ever—'future' relative to God's perspective, for God has no such perspective. God is only ever aware of the temporal relations between events in absolute terms. God is aware of the order in which various events occur—for example, God knows that you take your dog for a walk the day after you read this paragraph—but on the atemporalist picture God does not cognize this event as occurring in the past or the future. To return to the analogy that we introduced earlier in the chapter, God's knowledge of the temporal structure of our affairs is akin to our knowledge of the temporal structure of Tolkien's Middle Earth.

The atemporal conception of God may be able to resolve the tension between God's omniscience and free agency, but it faces a number of challenges in its own right. Some theorists have argued that it itself threatens God's omniscience, for there appear to be certain things that only a temporally located creature can know. Could an atemporal God know what time it is now? Many have argued not, on the grounds that one can grasp temporally indexed claims (such as 'It is now 9 a.m.') only if one is in time, and by hypothesis an atemporal God is not in time.

This objection to atemporalism is far from decisive; in fact, there are two plausible responses to it. For one thing, the atemporalist could simply accept that God doesn't know what time it is now. Adopting this response would involving giving up on God's omniscience (strictly speaking), but not in a way that would be religiously problematic. (After all, what precisely would the theist lose by admitting that God doesn't know the current time?) A second response would be to deny that there are genuinely indexical facts (such as facts about what time it is now). There are certainly indexical *representations* of time, but that doesn't entail that there are distinctively indexical *facts* about time. Arguably, any fact that can be represented indexically can also be represented non-indexically. Suppose, for example, that you ask yourself, 'What time it is now?' on 1 January 2018. Arguably, this fact is captured by the non-indexical proposition, 'On 1 January 2018 you asked yourself, "What time is it now?"', and even an atemporal God could know *that* proposition. In other words, the atemporalist might grant that although certain ways of representing temporal facts are unavailable to God, there are no temporal facts that are beyond God's ken.

A second objection to atemporalism is rather more serious. The objection in question is that atemporalism is difficult to reconcile with the claim that God is personal. As the philosopher Grace Jantzen has put it, 'A timeless and immutable God could not be personal because he could not create or respond, perceive or act, think, remember, or do any of the other things which persons do which require time.' There are, of course, many religious traditions in which God *is* thought of impersonally. For example, there are elements of ancient Greek thought in which God is regarded as more akin to an impersonal force than a personal being, and impersonal conceptions of God can also be found in certain strands of Hinduism and Daoism. But the central monotheistic religions—Judaism, Christianity, and Islam—are strongly committed to the view that God is both an agent and a subject of experience, and it is far from clear how an atemporal God could have these attributes.

Worship

Theists do not merely regard God as the creator of the world and as a being of unlimited knowledge, power, and goodness, they also conceive of God as the proper object of our worship. Indeed, not only do theists maintain that we ought to worship God, they typically think that God ought to be the *exclusive* object of our worship. But although worship is absolutely central to theism, it has not received a great deal of attention from philosophers. This is somewhat surprising, for worship raises a great many philosophical questions. Why might we be required to worship

God? What might ground our obligations to worship God? Indeed, what precisely *is* it to worship God?

One of the most influential discussions of worship is due to the philosopher James Rachels (1941–2003). Rachels argues that there is something deeply problematic in the idea that we ought to worship God. In fact, he argues that worship furnishes the materials for an objection to the very existence of God. He argues as follows:

(1) If any being is God, then that being must be a fitting object of worship.
(2) No being could possibly be a fitting object of worship, since worship requires the abandonment of one's role as an autonomous moral agent.
(3) Therefore, there cannot be a God.

Rachels' point is that even if the world was created by a being of perfect goodness, unlimited power, and so on, such a being would not qualify as the God of theism for we would have no obligation to worship it—indeed, it would not even be *appropriate* for us to worship it. The key step in the argument is premise (2)—the claim that worship is incompatible with autonomous moral agency. What should we make of it?

Some theists might be tempted by the view that if worship requires abandoning one's role as a moral agent then so much the worse for moral agency. But most theists, I suspect, will be reluctant to adopt that response, and will seek to reconcile the demands of worship with those of moral agency. Is that difficult to do? Rachels certainly thinks so: 'The worshiper's commitment to God has priority over any other commitments which he might have. But the first commitment of a moral agent is to do what in his own heart he thinks is right.' He elaborates on this point by invoking the story of the 'binding' of Isaac (Genesis 22), in which God commands Abraham to sacrifice his own son Isaac

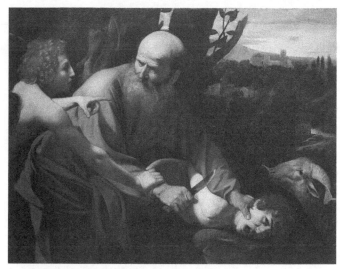

2. Caravaggio's 'Sacrifice of Isaac'.

(see Figure 2). Although Abraham does not go through with the sacrifice—at the last minute God provides a ram as a substitute for Isaac—Abraham is lauded by the Judeo-Christian tradition for his willingness to obey God. Rachels denies that Abraham's actions were those of an autonomous moral agent, for Abraham was willing to do what God commanded even though those commands were at odds with the dictates of his own moral compass.

Does Abraham really abdicate his responsibilities as a moral agent? The theist might point out that Abraham had to evaluate the source of this putative command: did it really derive from God, or might it have had another source (such as another agent, or even his own imagination)? And in making this assessment—the theist might continue—Abraham needed to engage his capacity for moral agency. Thus, far from undermining the exercise of moral agency, worship may actually require its deployment.

Is this response fully convincing? I certainly don't think that Rachels would be convinced by it. Even if determining the source of this putative command required Abraham to exercise his capacity for moral deliberation, having established that the command came from God the demands of worship then required Abraham to obey it, even though this command was at odds with what he himself took to be right. It is this fact, Rachels would argue, that undermines moral agency.

But there is perhaps an even deeper tension between the demands of worship and those of moral autonomy than the one that we have just considered. The tension in question concerns the self-conception that is implicit in any act of worship. Worship involves the affirmation of God's greatness and one's relative worthlessness, and it is precisely this attitude that many take to be at odds with human dignity. Of course, the theist will hold that there is nothing inappropriate about affirming one's relative worthlessness with respect to God, for the theist views such an affirmation as reflecting the true nature of things: we *are* relatively worthless when measured against the majesty of God.

At this point we reach the limit of argument, for there is no neutral perspective from which to adjudicate this dispute. Rachels' point of view is encapsulated in Frederick Nietzsche's rejection of theistic values: 'In God a declaration of hostility toward life, nature, and the will to life! In God nothingness deified, the will to nothingness sanctified!' The theist's point of view is in turn expressed by the Psalmist: 'What is man that you are mindful of him, and the son of man that you care for him?' (Psalm 8:4).

Chapter 3
Arguments for the existence of God

The ambitions of natural theology

Although religious authorities often laud the merits of faith, for many people proof is the bottom line when it comes to matters of belief. When asked what he would say if brought face to face with God in the afterlife, Bertrand Russell is reputed to have responded, 'Not enough evidence God! Not enough evidence!'

Is it possible to prove that God exists? There is certainly no shortage of arguments that purport to establish God's existence. Some arguments attempt to show that God's existence follows from the nature of consciousness; others attempt to show that God's existence follows from facts about morality; and still others attempt to show that God's existence follows from reports of miracles. Indeed, one famous argument for God's existence—the ontological argument—attempts to show that God's existence follows from the very concept of God.

We won't attempt to examine all of the arguments that have been offered for theism, but will instead focus on just three of the most influential arguments: the cosmological argument, the design argument, and the argument from religious experience. But before we examine these arguments, we need first to consider the very enterprise of attempting to establish God's existence.

What should we expect from an argument for God's existence? What would it take for such an argument to be successful?

The attempt to justify claims about the nature and existence of God on the basis of commonly accepted truths is known as natural theology. (Natural theology is contrasted with revealed theology: the latter appeals to the content of revelation, whereas the former appeals only to what can be established independently of revelation.) The advocates of natural theology have traditionally aimed to provide demonstrative proof for God's existence, where a proof is demonstrative if it leaves no room for rational doubt. This approach can be found in the work of Thomas Aquinas, for the arguments for God's existence that Aquinas gives are presented as having premises that will strike all rational individuals as self-evidently true, and which—if true—entail that God exists. Thus, to undermine Aquinas's arguments one need show only that the premises of his arguments can be rationally rejected, or that they fail to entail that God exists.

Although some theists still endorse the traditional aims of natural theology, most theists now assume that an argument for God's existence can be successful without being demonstrative. Contemporary theists do not typically require that the premises of a good argument for God's existence must strike all rational individuals as self-evidently true, nor do they require that these premises entail that God exists. Instead, they typically view an argument for God's existence as successful as long as its premises are generally compelling, and are such that they make it reasonable to think that God exists (or at least significantly raise the likelihood of God's existence). In these respects, arguments for God's existence can be likened to the arguments that one finds in science and the law. Scientists and lawyers don't typically aim to prove their claims beyond any shadow of doubt, but instead aim to show only that those claims are 'likely', 'probable', or perhaps 'beyond reasonable doubt'. Similarly, one might think that an argument for God's existence is successful if it shows that God's existence is 'likely', 'probable', or 'beyond reasonable doubt'. The question is whether there are any such arguments.

Cosmological arguments

One venerable family of arguments for God's existence are known as 'cosmological arguments'. Cosmological arguments attempt to argue for the existence of God from the mere existence of the cosmos. In effect, they appeal to God's activity as providing the best—or perhaps the only—explanation for why there is something rather than nothing. Prominent advocates of the cosmological argument include al-Ghazali (1058–1111), Ibn Rushd (1126–98), Maimonides (1138–1204), Thomas Aquinas, and G.W. Leibniz (1646–1716). Although the argument is not as popular as it once was, it continues to have its proponents.

There are two versions of the cosmological argument, an atemporal version and a temporal version.

The *temporal* version—which is often referred to as the *'kalām* argument' in honour of its Arabic roots (*'kalām'* is the Arabic term for 'word' or 'speech')—can be formulated as follows:

1. The universe began to exist.
2. Everything that begins to exist has a cause of its existence.
3. The universe has a cause of its existence. (From (1) and (2).)
4. If the universe has a cause, then that cause must be personal—that is, it must be God.
5. Therefore, there is a God.

Much of the discussion surrounding this argument has focused on (1)—the claim that the universe began to exist. Some advocates of the *kalām* argument defend (1) on the grounds that it would be incoherent to suppose that past time has been infinite. For example, al-Ghazali (Figure 3) argued that if past time were

3. Ahmad al-Ghazali addressing some youths. A miniature painting
from a 16th-century manuscript of the *Majalis al-'Ushshaq* ('The
Assemblies of the Lovers'). Image taken from Majalis al-'Ushshaq
of Sultan Husayn Mirza. Originally published/produced in Shiraz,
Iran, 1590–1600.

infinite then Saturn and Jupiter would have completed the same number of revolutions. But—al-Ghazali argued—Saturn and Jupiter obviously wouldn't complete the same number of revolutions in any given period of time, for Jupiter completes a revolution in twelve years whereas it takes Saturn thirty years to complete a revolution. Thus, he concluded, past time cannot be infinite.

This line of reasoning is ingenious, but it falls prey to a common confusion that arises when dealing with infinite sets. Consider the relationship between the even numbers (2, 4, 6, and so on) and the whole numbers (1, 2, 3, and so on). One might think that the set of even numbers must be smaller than the set of whole numbers on the grounds that the set of even numbers is a proper part of the set of whole numbers. However, mathematicians regard both sets as having the same size, for it is possible to establish a one-to-one correspondence between the members of the sets (2 can be mapped onto 1, 4 can be mapped on to 2, 6 can be mapped on to 3, and so on). As this example shows, our intuitive ways of determining the sizes of sets leads us astray when dealing with infinities, and al-Ghazali's argument appears to succumb to this confusion. If past time has indeed been infinite, then Saturn and Jupiter must have completed the same number of revolutions, since each of Saturn's revolutions can be put into correspondence with one of Jupiter's revolutions, just as each even number can be put into correspondence with a distinct whole number.

But although al-Ghazali's argument seems to fail, other reasons can be given in support of (1), and in fact most advocates of the *kalām* argument appeal to the 'Big Bang' account of contemporary physics to motivate the claim that the universe had a beginning in time.

What about (2): the claim that things that begin to exist must have a cause of their existence? We certainly assume that there are causes for the existence of ordinary, macroscopic objects such as cabbages, kings, and kangaroos. However, (2) is very far from being axiomatic, for quantum theory seems to be committed to the possibility of uncaused events. Leaving that point to one side, we should certainly be cautious about assuming causal explanations when considering the Big Bang itself, for we are here considering the explanation of nothing less than the universe itself, and it is unclear whether the very existence of the universe is something that has a causal explanation.

A further challenge to the argument concerns premise (4). Even if we grant that the universe began to exist, and that there must have been a cause of its existence, it is a further question whether this cause must have been an agent, let alone the kind of agent that might be a fitting object of religious devotion. Indeed, to the extent that the idea of an atemporal cause is intelligible, it would seem to point in the direction of impersonal entities and forces (such as gravity) rather than a personal agent, for personal agency seems to require temporality.

Let us turn now to *atemporal* versions of the cosmological argument. Instead of appealing to God to explain why the universe came into existence, atemporal cosmological arguments appeal to God to explain why the world (understood here as the sum of all concrete objects, minus God) exists at all.

One of the most influential forms of this argument begins with the apparent contingency of the world. The world clearly does exist, but it seems coherent to suppose that it might not have existed. But if the world's non-existence was possible then—advocates of this argument hold—its existence requires explanation, and the best—indeed, perhaps the only—explanation that can be offered must appeal to an entity whose existence is not contingent—in other words, God.

The argument can be formulated as follows:

(1) The universe is contingent.
(2) There is an explanation for the existence of all contingent entities.
(3) The existence of contingent entities can be explained only by appeal to a necessary being.
(4) There is at least one necessary being. (From (1), (2), and (3).)
(5) That necessary being is God.

This argument begins on solid footing, for its first premise is certainly plausible. Abstract entities such as numbers seem to exist necessarily, but particular concrete individuals—cabbages, kings, and kangaroos, not to mention you and me—seem to be contingent. Indeed, the universe as a whole seems also to be contingent. (Again, taking 'the universe' to refer to the sum of all concrete entities other than God.) In other words, it seems to be entirely possible that there might have been nothing.

Premise (1) of the argument seem reasonable—but what about (2)? Why assume that there is an explanation for why there is something rather than nothing? Why should we not treat the existence of things as a brute fact—something that has no explanation?

I think the fundamental appeal of (2) derives from what the philosopher Robert Nozick has called 'the presumption in favor of nothingness'. The idea is that 'inhabited' worlds (that is, worlds that contain things) pose explanatory questions that are not posed by 'empty' worlds (that is, worlds containing nothing—not even time or space). Given the presumption of nothingness, the existence of the actual world cries out for explanation.

The presumption of nothingness is attractive, but it is not uncontroversial. Some theorists argue that the very idea of empty worlds is incoherent; others argue that although empty worlds are possible, their likelihood is as close to zero as to be indistinguishable from it. The issues raised by these claims are complicated, and we must set them to one side here. What we can note, however, is that even if there is a presumption in favour of nothingness, it is a further question whether there is an explanation for why there is something rather than nothing.

The presumption of nothingness tells us that the default state of reality, so to speak, is that of non-existence, and thus that the existence of contingent entities requires an explanation. But it does not follow from this that there *is* an explanation for the existence of contingent entities. In order to bridge this gap we need to assume the truth of what is known as the *Principle of Sufficient Reason* (PSR): everything that stands in need of an explanation has an explanation. Philosophers have spilt a great deal of ink over PSR—some defend it; others reject it. Commitment to PSR appears to require that the universe is fundamentally intelligible, a claim that is by no means obviously true.

What about premise (3)—the claim that the existence of contingent entities can be explained only by appeal to a necessary being? One objection to (3) is that we don't have a good grasp of *how* the actions of a necessary being such as God might account for the existence of contingent entities. If we had a conception of how it is that an immaterial God could both create and sustain the world then (3) might be justified, but it is far from clear that we do have such a conception. Positing the existence of a necessary being does not itself provide any kind of explanation for how (or why) the world is populated with contingent entities.

A final objection to the cosmological argument is that God's existence seems to pose explanatory problems of its own. After all, if the existence of contingent beings needs to be explained, why doesn't God's existence also need to be explained? Advocates of the cosmological argument claim that God's existence doesn't need to be explained in the way in which the existence of the world does because God exists necessarily. There are ways things could have been such that you or I failed to exist, but—so the claim goes—there are no ways that things could have been such that God did not exist. But could a concrete being, such as God, exist necessarily? It is one thing for abstract objects such as numbers and propositions to exist necessarily, but it is quite another to ascribe necessary existence to a concrete particular. After all, ordinary entities (such as you and me) are regarded as contingent because we can conceive of their non-existence. But intuitions of contingency are not limited to ordinary concrete particulars (such as cabbages, kings, and kangaroos) but seem also to apply to any concrete entity whatsoever, including God (if there is a God).

In sum, the atemporal version of the cosmological argument would seem to be no more compelling than the temporal version. The fact that there is something rather than nothing is indeed deeply mysterious, but invoking God does little to dispel that mystery.

Design arguments

Although cosmological arguments continue to attract philosophical attention, it is design arguments—or rather, one particular version of the design argument—that occupies centre stage in the contemporary philosophy of religion. Design arguments—also known as 'teleological arguments' (from *telos*, the Greek word for 'design' or 'purpose')—have featured in philosophical discussion since the time of the ancient Greeks. Indeed, a particularly eloquent version of the argument can be found in Cicero's *On the Nature of the Gods*, in which Cicero puts the following words into the mouth of a Stoic philosopher:

> When we see something moved by machinery, like an orrery
> or clock or many other such things, we do not doubt that these
> contrivances are the work of reason; when therefore we behold the
> whole compass of the heaven moving with revolutions of marvelous
> velocity and executing with perfect regularity the annual changes of

the seasons with absolute safety and security for all things, how can
we doubt that all this is effected not merely by reason, but by a
reason that is transcendent and divine?

Cicero's Stoic spokesman goes on to claim that it is not only celestial
order that points to the existence of a divine architect, but that
various forms of biological order are also evidence of cosmic design.

How skillful and exact is the disposition of the various parts of [the
bodies of animals], how marvelous the structure of the limbs. For
all the organs ... are so formed and so placed that none of them is
superfluous or not necessary for the preservation of life.

Although biological versions of the design argument remained
popular into well into the 19th century, their prospects were dealt
a fatal blow in 1859 with the publication of Charles Darwin's *On
the Origin of Species*. What Darwin suggested—and the subsequent
development of evolutionary science has confirmed—is that it is
possible to explain both the complexity of organisms and the fact
that they are so often well-suited to their environments without
appealing to intelligent design.

But the demise of biological versions of the design argument
did not mark the demise of the design argument as such, and
in recent decades the argument has undergone a remarkable
renaissance. Contemporary advocates of the design argument
appeal not to the kinds of structure studied in the biological
sciences but to the more fundamental forms of structure that
characterize the cosmos as a whole.

Some theorists focus on the fact that the world exhibits temporal
regularities—in other words, that there are laws of nature. Consider
the fact that water boils at 100 degrees centigrade at sea level.
This law held a century ago, it holds now, and we expect that it
will continue to hold come what may. The fact that the world
exhibits temporal regularities in this way is something that

cries out for explanation. Why is the universe not entirely lawless, exhibiting no temporal regularities whatsoever? Advocates of the design argument point out that science itself cannot explain why there are laws of nature; at best, science can explain some laws of nature by appealing to other, more fundamental, laws. In other words, to explain why nature exhibits regularities we must look beyond science; in particular—advocates of the design argument hold—we must appeal to the activity of an intelligent designer (in other words, God).

Although this version of the design argument is worthy of serious attention, we will set it to one side in order to examine a version of the design argument that focuses not on the existence of laws of nature as such, but on the fact that the laws of nature—together with various fundamental constants—appear to be 'fine-tuned' for life. Had these laws and fundamental constants been ever-so-slightly different, then intelligent life would not have occurred. Consider, for example, the cosmological constant, symbolized by the Greek letter 'Λ', which plays a crucial role in the theory of General Relativity. If Λ had a value that was even slightly different from its actual value, then either space would have expanded at such a rate that objects would not exhibit the stability they do, or the universe would have collapsed in on itself immediately after the Big Bang. In other words, Λ needed to have almost exactly the value that it actually has in order for the world to exhibit the kind of stability that appears to be required for intelligent life. Indeed, it has been suggested that the chances of Λ having this value are one in a trillion trillion trillion trillion. Many of the other fundamental physical constants—for example, the mass of the proton, the mass of the neutron, the speed of light, the Newtonian gravitational constant—also fall within the very narrow boundaries that appear to be required for the emergence of intelligent life. Many theorists argue that these facts—what we might call 'fine-tuning facts'—are evidence for the existence of a divine architect. For obvious reasons, this is known as the *fine-tuning* version of the cosmological argument.

As an analogy, consider the *Tale of the Expert Marksmen*. Suppose that the commander of the prison camp in which you are interned has ordered that you be executed by firing squad. You are marched into the middle of the camp, and although twelve expert marksmen each fire 1,000 bullets at you, you survive unscathed. What should you conclude? You could, of course, conclude that you were incredibly lucky, and that there is no rational explanation for why you have survived. However, it is surely more reasonable for you to conclude that the event was staged, and that—for reasons unknown to you—the commander ordered the guards to miss you. Similarly, the advocate of the fine-tuning argument argues that although you could conclude that we are incredibly luckily to live in a universe in which the fundamental constants fall within the boundaries that are required for intelligent life, it is surely more rational to conclude that the fine-tuning facts obtain precisely because the universe has been designed so as to ensure (or at least allow for) the emergence of intelligent life.

Four claims underpin the fine-tuning argument. The first claim is that the fine-tuning facts need explaining. The second claim is that these facts lack a scientific explanation. The third claim is that an appeal to intelligent design would provide a good explanation for the fine-tuning facts. And the fourth claim is that an appeal to God's creative activity would provide a better explanation of the fine-tuning facts than explanations that appeal to other forms of intelligent design. One can regard each claim as homing in on a God-shaped gap: one first establishes the existence of a genuine explanatory gap; one then argues that this gap cannot be filled by science; one then argues that it can be filled by a designer; finally, one argues that this designer is God. Let us consider each of these steps in turn.

Some have argued that the fine-tuning facts don't represent a genuine explanatory challenge, and that the only phenomena to be explained here are not the fine-tuning facts themselves, but why we find these facts surprising. After all—this line of thought continues—it is no wonder that the fine-tuning facts obtain, for if they failed to obtain then we wouldn't be here to pose the kinds of questions that lie behind the fine-tuning argument.

This objection seems to me to be misguided. It is certainly true that our existence entails that the preconditions for intelligent life have been met. But it hardly follows from this that the obtaining of the fine-tuning facts was itself necessary, or that it is not in any way surprising. (Compare: it is necessarily the case that if I have had breakfast today then I have eaten today, but it is not the case that my eating today was necessary.) Recall the *Tale of the Expert Marksmen*. It is certainly true that the protagonist at the centre of this tale cannot reflect on the reasons for his survival unless he does in fact survive—this is what is known as an 'observational selection effect'—but that doesn't make his survival any less surprising or in need of explanation. Similarly, the fact that our existence presupposes the very facts that are under investigation in no way shows that those facts do not require explanation.

Let us grant, then, that the fine-tuning facts require explanation. Can science provide the necessary explanation? Many physicists and philosophers argue that it can. The most influential response here appeals to the 'many worlds' or 'multiverse' hypothesis. The basic idea is this. The existence of a finely tuned world would be surprising given the assumption that there is only one universe, but it may not be surprising if our universe is only one of a vast (perhaps infinite) number of universes, each of which exhibits variation in the values of the basic physical constants. If the multiverse hypothesis were correct, then—this line of thought continues—we would have a purely scientific explanation for the fine-tuning facts. Although the vast majority of universes fail to support life, occasionally the fundamental constants are such that intelligent life becomes possible. Our world just happens to be such a world. We might liken the multiverse scenario to a scenario in which the expert marksmen don't shoot just one prisoner, but fire at a vast (perhaps infinite) number of prisoners. In such a scenario, one might expect that although the vast majority of prisoners will die, occasionally someone survives, and of course it's only the survivors who are in a position to reflect on their luck.

Note that the multiverse hypothesis doesn't raise the probability that this particular universe is fit for life. Instead, by representing this universe as merely one of a multitude of universes it attempts to make this fact less mysterious, and thus less in need of the kind of explanation offered by the fine-tuning argument. The astronomer Martin Rees suggests an analogy with an 'off-the-shelf' clothing store: 'if the shop has a large stock we're not surprised to find a suit that fits. Likewise, if our universe is selected from a multiverse, its seemingly designed or fine-tuned features wouldn't be surprising.'

Would it be surprising that it is *this* universe that is fine-tuned for life? No, for the only thing that is special about this universe is that it contains intelligent life, and of course this universe contains intelligent life only because the fine-tuning facts obtain in it.

The question, of course, is whether the multiverse hypothesis *is* true. Some have been tempted to argue that the very existence of the fine-tuning facts provides evidence for the multiverse hypothesis. They reason that if this universe were the only one of its kind then those facts would be surprising, and hence that it is reasonable to conclude that this universe must be one of many universes. Critics charge that this line of argument is guilty of what is called the Inverse Gambler's Fallacy, which is the fallacy of assuming that because an event is unlikely it must be one of a series of events. (An example: Suppose that you walk into a casino and see a gambler roll a double six. You commit the Inverse Gambler's Fallacy if you assume that because a double six is unlikely, that roll must have been only one of many rolls that the gambler has made.) Other advocates of the multiverse hypothesis appeal to the many-worlds interpretation of quantum mechanics, arguing that the existence of many universes follows from the best account of quantum phenomena. The debate regarding the appropriate interpretation of quantum mechanics is on-going, and it is unclear what the status of the multiverse hypothesis will be when the dust settles. Perhaps all that can be said at the moment is that the prospects for providing a scientific explanation of the fine-tuning facts remain uncertain.

Let us turn now to the third of the four claims on which the fine-tuning argument rests. Would an appeal to intelligent design provide a *good* explanation of the fine-tuning facts? Indeed, would it provide any kind of explanation of these facts at all?

There are three possible reasons for doubt. The first concerns the obscurity surrounding the notion of divine creation (see also Chapter 2). Our own agency certainly does not encompass the capacity to alter the fundamental structure of the physical world. No doubt there are possible beings whose capacity to control matter vastly exceeds that of our own, but it's far from clear that any kind of being could alter the laws of nature or fix the values of the fundamental physical constants. The theist might respond by suggesting that the nature of God's creative activity is a mystery, but that response would be unconvincing in this context, for we are here evaluating an argument for God's existence the very cogency of which assumes the legitimacy of appealing to God's creative activity. How could that argument be convincing if we have no grasp of how God might have created the world?

Second, even if there are agents who are able to alter the fundamental physical constants, we can appeal to their activity to explain the fine-tuning facts only if we are entitled to assume that they would have been motivated to create a finely tuned world. A number of theorists have argued that we are not entitled to make that assumption. In the words of Stephen Jay Gould, 'If disembodied mind does exist (and I'll be damned if I know of any source of scientific evidence for or against such an idea), must it prefer a universe that will generate our earth's style of life, rather than a cosmos filled with diprotons?' The philosopher J.J.C. Smart coined the phrase 'psychocentric hubris' to describe the assumption that beings with the capacity to create a world like ours would want to do so. *We* might be motivated to create a universe much like the actual one, but why assume that our motivations would be shared by the kinds of creatures with the capacity to create worlds?

Despite the popularity of this objection, I myself am not much impressed by it. For one thing, the advocate of the fine-tuning argument isn't committed to the claim that any creator would, of necessity, bring about a world containing human beings, or even that it would be compelled to create a world containing intelligent life of any kind. Rather, the argument requires only that the creation of intelligent life would be something that a world-maker is likely to do—something that it wouldn't be terribly surprising for it to do. It seems to me that this is not an implausible assumption. After all, it is not unreasonable to suppose that intelligence and the kinds of capacities that it makes possible—friendship, love, creativity—are objective goods. Certainly anyone who recoils in horror at the idea that intelligent life might be annihilated by a nuclear holocaust should deny that the fine-tuning argument rests on nothing more than psychocentric hubris.

A third reason to doubt whether fine-tuning facts could justify the hypothesis of an intelligent designer is, in my view, much more weighty. Indeed, I regard this objection as one of the most profound in all of the philosophy of religion. The objection has its roots in a question posed by David Hume: 'Why should we not suppose an animal body to be ordered and organized originally, of itself, or from unknown causes, than in supposing a mind to be ordered in that way?' We might put Hume's point this way. Think of reality as containing two types of structures: physical structure and mental structure. Design arguments focus on

40

physical structure, and invoke the structure of God's mind to explain the structure of the physical world. As such, they treat mental structure as an unexplained explainer. But—Hume asks—why should we not treat physical structure as an unexplained explainer? Do we have any reason to think that mental phenomena are inherently structured whereas physical phenomena are not? In other words, do we have any reason to think that physical structure requires explanation in a way that mental structure does not? Hume's answer—which seems to me to be exactly right—is that we don't. But if that is right, then no argument which assumes that mental structure is more fundamental than physical structure (as the design argument does) can succeed.

Let us turn, finally, to the fourth claim that underpins the fine-tuning argument—and indeed any version of the design argument. Assuming that the advocate of the argument can show that the cosmos was the result of creative intelligence, what reason might she have for identifying that intelligence with the God of theism?

We are again indebted to Hume for making this challenge vivid, for in his *Dialogues Concerning Natural Religion* Hume suggests a number of alternatives to the theistic claim that the world was created by a single being of perfect goodness and power. Perhaps, Hume suggests, the world was the 'first rude essay of some infant deity, who afterwards abandoned it, ashamed of his lame performance.' Perhaps it was the work of some 'superannuated deity in its dotage', or a 'dependent, inferior deity; and is the object of derision to his superiors'. Perhaps, Hume adds, the world was produced by a committee of cosmic architects. To Hume's list we can add any number of others possibilities. Perhaps the world was brought into being by an advanced race, who have created us for the amusement of their children. Perhaps it resulted from a bug in a super-computer that was designed to make industrial-strength disinfectant. Perhaps we are the result of a glitch in some kind of

41

cosmic photocopier. The point in mentioning these proposals is not to defend them as serious accounts of the origin of the world, but to point out that even if we accept that the world is the result of intelligent design, the theistic hypothesis is only one of many hypotheses that might be considered. (We might also note that many of these hypotheses provide straightforward explanations for why the world seems to be largely indifferent to our well-being—and indeed to the well-being of sentient creatures in general—whereas theism struggles to account for this fact.)

Some advocates of the design argument, such as Richard Swinburne and William Lane Craig, argue that theism is simpler than any of these alternatives, and is thus to be preferred because the simplicity of a hypothesis is a mark in its favour. I find this response unconvincing. Not only is it far from clear that theism *is* simpler than its rivals, the fact is that there are a great many—perhaps uncountably many—alternatives to theism. So, even if the inherent likelihood of theism were (say) a million times higher than that of any one of its rivals, it is still much less likely that theism is true than it is that one or another of its rivals is true.

In my view a much better response to Hume's objection is to grant that the design argument doesn't take one all the way to the God of theism, and that at best it can establish only that the universe had an architect of some kind or other. The case for identifying that architect with the God of theism would then need to be made on independent grounds, involving (say) an appeal to other arguments for God's existence or the content of divine revelation. Although this version of the design argument is certainly less ambitious than many that have been advanced, its success would be far from negligible. The question, of course, is whether even this relatively modest version of the argument can overcome the objections that we have considered.

The argument from religious experience

The French philosopher and mathematician Blaise Pascal (1623–62; Figure 4) had little time for the alleged proofs of God's existence, complaining that they are

> so remote from human reasoning and so involved that they make little impact, and, even if they did help some people, it would only be for a moment during which they watched the demonstration, because an hour later they would be afraid that they had made a mistake.

Pascal's comments were directed at the 'metaphysical' proofs for God's existence, such as the cosmological and design arguments. There is, however, an argument for God's existence that is not remote from human reasoning: the argument from religious experience.

4. Blaise Pascal.

Religious experiences are common. A recent survey of Americans found that nearly half of all respondents (49 per cent) claimed to have had a 'moment of sudden religious insight or awakening'. Not surprisingly, the proportion of individuals reporting such experiences was higher among those who identified as religious, but even 30 per cent of respondents with no religious affiliation claimed to have had religious experiences. Pascal himself seems to have had a religious experience. After his death a piece of parchment that had been sewn into his coat was discovered, on which was inscribed a record of an event that had occurred to him on the evening of 23 November 1654, with the words 'Fire—God of Abraham, God of Isaac, God of Jacob, not of philosophers and scholars'.

Before we turn to the argument from religious experience, we need to distinguish two ways in which the phrase 'religious experience' can be used. In one sense of the term, an experience qualifies as religious only if it has actually put one in touch with a religious reality of some kind. Although some theorists use the phrase 'religious experience' in this way, I use it in a less committal sense, according to which a religious experience is an experience in which one *seems* to have been in touch with a religious reality of some kind. In this sense of the term, the existence of religious experiences doesn't require that there is indeed a religious reality of any kind.

There are various forms of religious experience. Some religious experiences involve ordinary objects taking on a religious significance, as when a sacred building or a sublime landscape elicits a sense of transcendent reality. Some religious experiences involve visual or auditory experiences that seem to have a religious origin, as when one sees a heavenly vision or hears what one takes to be the voice of God. Although experiences of these kinds raise interesting philosophical questions, discussions of religious experience within the philosophy of religion tend to focus on a third class of religious experiences: experiences in which God seems to be directly present to one. The central question here is whether such experiences can generate reasons for belief in God.

The philosopher William Alston (1921–2009) argued that they can. At the heart of Alston's case is the claim that there is a deep commonality between religious experiences and ordinary perceptual experiences, such as your visual experiences of this book. Those who have religious experiences, Alston claims, typically take God to have been presented to their consciousness 'in generically the same way as that in which objects in the environment are presented to one's consciousness in sense perception'. Alston goes on to argue that religious experiences have the same epistemic status that perceptual experiences have: they are *prima facie* trustworthy—innocent unless proven guilty. Although the senses do occasionally deceive us (consider dreams, illusions, and hallucinations), we are justified in taking the experiences that they generate at face value unless we have reason to think that we are being misled in some way. Similarly, Alston argues, we are justified in taking religious experiences at face value unless we have reason to think that we are being misled in some way. And, he argues, since we do not always have reason to think that we are being misled, it follows that religious experiences sometimes justify belief in the existence of God.

Objections to Alston's position can be divided into two classes. One sort of objection holds that there are crucial differences between religious experiences and ordinary perceptual experiences, such that religious experience shouldn't be regarded as a form of perceptual experience. Another kind of objection holds that even if religious experiences qualify as a kind of perceptual experience, they lack the epistemic status that standard perceptual experiences enjoy. Let us begin with challenges to the claim that religious experiences could qualify as perceptual.

Suppose that you are at a party, and you happen to see the President of Tajikistan help himself to a glass of champagne. Although the person that you see is the President of Tajikistan, you don't see him *as* the President of Tajikistan. Your experience is an experience *of* the President of Tajikistan, but there is nothing in your visual experience which reveals the identity of the man that you see; your experience does not furnish you with a reason to believe that you are looking at the President of Tajikistan. Similarly, the objection runs, even if your experience is an experience *of* God, there is nothing in your experience itself that reveals the identity of its object. Your experience is not an experience of God *as* God. In order for your religious experience to be an experience of God as such, the argument continues, you would need to be able to experience God as having those properties that are essential to God's nature, such as being the creator of the world. But—the objection continues—these properties are no more perceptible than is the property of being the President of Tajikistan. Since Alston's argument clearly requires the existence of experiences in which it is manifest in the experience itself that it is an experience of God, the argument fails.

What should we make of this objection? We should certainly grant that many of the properties that theists take to be essential to God's nature cannot be experienced. One cannot experience God as the creator of the cosmos, nor can one experience God as unlimited in knowledge, power, and goodness. But the objection overlooks the fact that God might have other distinctive properties that are perhaps experientially detectable. Time and again those who have religious experiences describe the object of their experience as 'holy', 'awesome', and 'transcendent.' It is presumably these aspects of their religious experiences—what Rudolf Otto described as their 'noumenal' aspects—which explains why so many individuals are convinced that their experiences are experiences of God.

A second—and in my view more serious—objection to the view that religious experiences might qualify as perceptual concerns the fact that perception involves a kind of causal sensitivity to an object and its properties. If the orientation or colour of this book were to change, then your visual experience of it would also change in predictable ways. It is this causal sensitivity that lies at the basis of perception's evidential role. Thus, if religious experiences are perceptual experiences then they too must exhibit this kind of causal sensitivity. But—the objection continues—it is unclear how they could exhibit causal sensitivity given that God is not spatially located. After all, other non-spatial entities—such as numbers and propositions—are not possible objects of perceptual experience, in part precisely because we cannot be causally related to them. You can perceive representations of numbers (that is, numerals), but you cannot perceive numbers themselves.

Alston denies that there is any real difficulty here, arguing that because God is the causal ground of everything that occurs, it follows that God can cause religious experiences. However, it is not clear whether this response is fully convincing, for even if we grant that God is the causal ground of all that exists, God's causal contribution to religious experiences might fail to be the kind of causal contribution that is required by the causal condition on perception. As the philosopher Nick Zangwill has pointed out, the Big Bang is in some sense a cause of your current visual experiences (if the Big Bang hadn't occurred then you wouldn't exist), but it hardly follows that you can perceive the Big Bang. Zangwill's point is that perception requires more than a 'but for' cause ('I wouldn't have existed but for the Big Bang'), and thus the fact that God might be a 'but for' cause of religious experiences fails to show that religious experiences can meet the causal constraint on perception.

Let us assume, if only for the sake of argument, that religious experiences qualify as perceptual states. Might they inherit the epistemic status of perceptual states, and thus justify beliefs in the way that perceptual experiences can? At least three reasons have been given for answering this question in the negative.

The first reason concerns experiences of God's absence. Some critics argue that if experiences of God's presence provide evidence *for* God's existence, then experiences of God's absence (which are arguably no less common) ought, by parity of reasoning, to provide evidence *against* God's existence. Thus, this objection runs, the evidential force of religious experiences would be cancelled out by the evidential force of what we might call 'a-religious' experiences.

This objection overlooks the fact that experiences of presence are not normally on a par with experiences of absence. Spotting a friend in a crowd provides one with a reason to think that she has made it to the party, but failing to spot her doesn't in the same way provide one with a reason to think that she has failed to turn up. Of course, there are conditions in which experiences of absence can justify beliefs. If one were entitled to assume that if one's friend were present then one would have seen her, then failing to see her might provide one with a reason to think that she is absent. (Suppose that the party is a small one, and one is sure that one would have seen one's friend if she were there.) Similarly, if one were entitled to assume that if God exists then one would have experienced God, then experiences of God's absence might provide one with a reason to think that God doesn't exist. But are we entitled to that assumption? There are various ways in which such an assumption might be defended, but it is clear that any such defence would be controversial.

A second reason to deny that religious experiences have the same epistemic status as ordinary perceptual experiences involves the claim that the epistemic status of perception depends on a grasp of the conditions under which perceptual experiences are trustworthy. Consider, again, vision. One doesn't need a degree in vision science to know that vision is more trustworthy in some conditions (when the scene is appropriately illuminated; when one is attentive and alert) than in others (when the scene is poorly lit; when one is tired or drowsy). In other words, we have some capacity to distinguish contexts in which visual experiences are trustworthy from those in which they are untrustworthy. But—the objection runs—we have no corresponding capacity to distinguish contexts in which religious experiences are likely to be trustworthy from those in which they are likely to be untrustworthy, for we don't know what conditions affect the reliability of religious experience.

The nature of this problem can be appreciated by considering drug-induced experiences. We know that drug-induced *visual* experiences are not to be trusted, but what about drug-induced *religious* experiences? Are the religious experiences that are triggered by ingesting psychedelics less trustworthy than those that occur in the absence of drugs? How would one tell? Perhaps drug-induced religious experiences are *more* trustworthy than those occur in the absence of drugs. Perhaps the fact that a religious experience was triggered by psychedelics has no impact at all on its trustworthiness. Not only are the answers to these questions obscure, it is unclear how one might even begin to go about addressing them. The fundamental problem here is that our ability to distinguish trustworthy experiences from untrustworthy ones depends on our capacity to locate experiences within the causal structure of the world, and—for reasons that we have already noted—it is not clear how religious experiences can be so-located.

Let us consider one final challenge to the argument from religious experience: the challenge from religious pluralism. Although religious experiences can be found within all cultures, their contents seem to differ in fundamental ways from one context to another. As the critic Michael Martin has put it, 'religious experiences in one culture often conflict with those in another. One cannot accept all of them as veridical, yet there does not seem to be a way to separate the veridical experiences from the rest.' The objection allows that although religious experiences could in principle justify belief in God's existence, in practice no such case can be made given the lack of coherence exhibited by the variety of religious experiences that actually occur. As an analogy, consider a world in which the visual experiences of one group of people were starkly at odds with those of another group, so that inter-subjective agreement about how to describe the objects of sight was rare if not altogether absent. In such a world, one might well doubt whether visual experience was a form of contact with an objective, mind-independent world, as opposed to a mere play of subjective impressions.

This is surely one of the most powerful objections to the argument from religious experience. Some theorists respond to it by suggesting that the conflict between religious experiences is merely superficial, and that underlying the obvious disagreement is a set of core contents that is common to all religious experiences. (An analogy: eye-witnesses to a robbery might give different descriptions of what the robber was wearing, but they might all agree that the robber was male.) But if there is a common core to religious experiences giving an account of its content is far from straightforward. For example, some individuals describe their religious experiences in personal terms, claiming to have communed with another mind, whereas others describe their experiences in impersonal terms, claiming to have attained a state of union with the Absolute. It is difficult to see what substantive content these two kinds of experiences might have in common.

There is no denying that religious experiences provide moments of deep meaning and fulfilment to many. For some they are a source of solace; for others they are life-changing. The considerations provided here in no way belittle the role that religious experience play in the life of faith, but they do raise questions about whether such experiences can ground a compelling argument for God's existence.

Does it matter?

Although it is certainly possible to find intelligent, well-informed, and reflective individuals who regard one or more of the arguments for God's existence as persuasive, I'm inclined to agree with John Cottingham's verdict:

> it seems unlikely that any of the arguments for God's existence could succeed in convincing any rational inquirer 'cold', as it were, in the way in which, say, a geometrical proof in Euclid must convince any attentive reader who carefully follows the axioms and deductions, or even in the way in which a proof of the solubility of gold in hydrochloric acid must be accepted by any reasonable observer who carefully examines the experimental evidence.

Suppose—if only for the sake of argument—that it is not possible to establish the existence of God beyond reasonable doubt. What would follow from this fact?

Some hold that the failure of natural theology would be a catastrophe for theism. They argue that if it is not possible to establish God's existence then the intellectual respectability of theism would be undermined, and belief in God would be unmasked as irrational at best and delusional at worst. Others regard the potential failure of natural theology with indifference, holding that religious belief ought to be independent of considerations of reason and rationality. Whether or not it is possible to prove that God exists, they claim, evidence and argument are irrelevant when it comes to questions of faith. A third group of theorists views the potential failure of natural theology as a cause for celebration on the part of those with religious commitments, for they regard proof as the enemy of faith. If God's existence were proved, they argue, then there would be no room for faith, and the loss of faith would bring with it the loss of much that is most valuable in religious life. I will leave you to consider which of these three positions is most attractive.

Chapter 4
Divine hiddenness and the nature of faith

The hiddenness objection

Writing towards the end of the 19th century, the German philosopher Frederick Nietzsche penned the following complaint against religion:

> A god who is all-knowing and all-powerful and who does not even make sure his creatures understand his intentions—could that be a god of goodness? Who allows countless doubts and dubieties to persist, for thousands of years, as though the salvation of mankind were unaffected by them, and who on the other hand holds out frightful consequences if any mistake is made as to the nature of truth.... Would he not be a cruel god if he possessed the truth and could behold mankind miserably tormenting itself over the truth?

Religious writers have long puzzled over the reasons for God's silence, but Nietzsche regarded the silence of God as something more than a pastoral challenge: he saw it as an objection to the very reasonableness of religious belief. Assuming—as theists invariably do—that God wants to be recognized and worshipped, why does God not make Godself manifest? Perhaps, Nietzsche suggests, God is 'silent' because God doesn't exist.

In recent years Nietzsche's challenge has been forcefully developed by the philosopher J.L. Schellenberg, who argues that the very fact that the evidence for God's existence is inconclusive is itself a strong reason for disbelief. The God of theism, he argues, would always be open to a personal relationship with us, and a precondition of that relationship is believing that God exists. 'If a perfectly loving God exists,' he writes, 'our situation will be one in which God's existence is beyond reasonable nonbelief for all who are capable of a personal relationship with God.'

Some will be inclined to reject the very starting point of the hiddenness objection, arguing that there is ample evidence of God's existence, and thus that God's existence is not beyond reasonable nonbelief. (Pascal may have been tempted by this thought: 'There is enough light for those who desire to see, and enough darkness for those of a contrary disposition.') But surely there is such a thing as reasonable nonbelief. As we saw in Chapter 3, no argument for God's existence commands general assent, and even those who claim that there are sound arguments for God's existence often disagree about which theistic arguments are sound. Appeals to revelation fare no better, for there is no consensus regarding which scriptures are authoritative. Some individuals regard God's existence as beyond reasonable doubt, but for many God's existence is a matter of mystery and obscurity. Indeed, an acknowledgement of the hiddenness of God is a prominent theme in the writings of many theists. In the words of the Swiss theologian Karl Barth: 'That God is, lies as little in the field of our spiritual oversight and control as what He is. We lack the capacity both to establish his existence, and to define his being.'

Atheists have a simple explanation for the silence of God. What explanation can theists provide?

The need for epistemic distance

Some explanations for divine hiddenness treat it as a purely undesirable state of affairs. One version of this account ascribes divine hiddenness to our cognitive deficiencies; another version ascribes it to the effects of sin. We will leave these explanations to one side here and consider instead those that focus on the benefits that are alleged to accrue from divine hiddenness.

One proposal in this vein is that divine hiddenness is a precondition for moral agency. Richard Swinburne captures this idea as follows:

> Knowing that there was a God, men would know that their most secret thoughts and actions were known to God; and knowing that he was just, they would expect for their bad actions and thoughts whatever punishment was just.... In such a world men would have little temptation to do wrong—it would be the mark of both prudence and reason to do what was virtuous.

If God's existence were evident to us, Swinburne argues, then our opportunities for exercising genuine moral freedom would be severely curtailed if not altogether eliminated.

This proposal can be challenged from a number of directions. For one thing, the idea that religious certainty leaves no room for temptation seems implausible, for those theists who regard God's existence as beyond doubt evidently remain subject to temptation. One might also challenge the assumption that the capacity to experience temptation is required for genuine moral agency. Theists have particular reason to question this claim, for they regard God as a moral agent but they typically deny that God is subject to temptation.

A second response to the hiddenness objection focuses on the idea that if God's existence were evident to us then any relationship that we might have with God would be inauthentic. Instead of embracing a religious way of life for its own sake, we would inevitably embrace it for purely instrumental reasons, treating God as an object to be manipulated for our own ends rather than as a being with whom we might enter into spiritual communion.

But why precisely would regarding God's existence as evident bring with it a coercive attitude? As we noted earlier, some theists take God's existence to be beyond reasonable doubt, but it is implausible to suppose that their attitude to God is necessarily coercive. Theists often liken God's relationship to humanity with the relationship that parents have to their children, but few parents conceal themselves behind a veil of uncertainty, hoping that their children might nevertheless come to believe in their existence. Instead, parents typically do everything in their power to make their existence and intentions manifest to their children. Why wouldn't a good God do likewise?

The appeal to faith

The two attempts to justify God's hiddenness that we have just considered focus on the drawbacks that are alleged to follow if God's existence were evident. A third response focuses on the alleged benefits that might be thought to accrue from divine hiddenness itself. Belief in God—so this line of thought goes—is more virtuous when it is based on faith, and if God's existence were evident then there would be no room for faith, for faith can flourish only in a climate of uncertainty and ambiguity.

Evaluating this response to the hiddenness objection will occupy us for the best part of this chapter, for the questions that it raises are some of the most fundamental in the philosophy of religion. Let us begin with one that is perhaps the most fundamental of all: What exactly is faith?

Mark Twain once quipped that faith is a matter of 'believing what you know ain't so'. Although few philosophers would endorse Twain's conception of faith, the idea that faith is a kind of belief is widely accepted. Consider the following passage from Thomas Aquinas's *Summa Theologica*:

In faith the intellect assents to something, not through being
sufficiently moved by its proper object, but through an act of choice,
whereby it turns voluntarily to one side rather than to the other: and
if this be accompanied by doubt and fear of the opposite side there
will be opinion, while if there be certainty and no fear of the other
side, there will be faith.

Let us call the view that religious faith is a matter of belief 'the
doxastic view'. (*Doxa* is the Greek for 'belief' or 'opinion'.)

Although the doxastic view has been influential, it is open to an
important challenge involving the idea that faith is subject to
moral evaluation. Having faith is something for which one can be
praised, whereas the lack of faith is something for which one can be
blamed. In order for the doxastic account to do justice to the moral
dimensions of faith, the formation of belief—'intellectual assent',
as Aquinas puts it—would need to involve an act of choice. But the
idea that we can choose what to believe is deeply problematic. The
Queen in Lewis Carroll's *Through the Looking-Glass* claimed to
have believed six impossible things before breakfast, but few of us
can manage that feat—indeed, few of us can choose to believe even
those claims that we regard as open questions. Consider a topic that
your current evidence leaves unsettled, such as whether there is
intelligent life on other planets. Do you turn to 'one side or another'
and adopt one answer rather than another through an act of choice?
I doubt it. Rather, I suspect that a certain answer simply strikes
you as more plausible than another. (And if no position strikes you
as plausible, you will simply suspend belief.) There are many things
that one can do to influence what one believes—for example, one
can choose to pursue one line of enquiry rather than another—but
belief as such does not seem to be under voluntary control.
Intellectual assent seems to be something that *happens* to us
rather than something that we *do*. But if that is right, then it isn't
meritorious, and we are no more to be praised (or blamed) for our
beliefs than we are for the circulation of our blood or the smooth
running of our kidneys.

This suggests that insofar as faith is subject to moral evaluation it cannot be a matter of belief. What might faith be if not a kind of belief? A number of alternatives have been proposed. Some have suggested that faith is a kind of hope; others that it is a kind of preference. Perhaps the most influential alternative to the doxastic view identifies faith with a form of trust (Figure 5). Thus understood, one can have faith in a person by deciding to employ them, and one can have faith in a relationship by deciding to forgo certain goods in order to sustain it. Indeed, this conception of faith—faith *in* rather than faith *that*—ought surely to resonate with members of the Abrahamic religions, for Abraham's faith centred on his willingness to trust God rather than on his belief in God's existence.

Where do these considerations leave the idea that an appeal to faith might explain why God might have chosen to remain 'hidden'? In fairly bad shape, it seems to me, for there could be ample space for religious faith (understood here as a matter of trust in God) without God's existence being shrouded in ambiguity

5. Colin McCahon's 'Scared', 1976.

and uncertainty. The story of Abraham illustrates this point with particular potency, for Abraham's (presumed) certainty in the existence of God did not mean that his faith in God wasn't put to the test.

Clifford and the ethics of belief

In addition to asking why God might permit divine hiddenness, we can also consider the implications of divine hiddenness for the ethics of religious belief. Many have argued that, given the ambiguity surrounding God's existence, theism is irresponsible if not altogether blameworthy. To believe in God, they argue, is to flout one's duties as a rational agent.

This challenge is associated with the work of the 'new atheists' such as Richard Dawkins, Sam Harris, and Christopher Hitchens, but its roots go back to an influential article by a Victorian Englishman named W.K. Clifford (1845–79) entitled 'The Ethics of Belief'. Clifford begins his essay with the tale of a ship-owner who sent his ship to sea despite a lack of evidence as to its sea-worthiness. According to Clifford, the owner was guilty of the deaths of those who perished when it sank, for he ought not to have believed that his ship was sea-worthy. Clifford draws a general moral from this tale: it is, he says, 'wrong always, everywhere, and for anyone, to believe anything upon insufficient evidence'. Although religious belief is not mentioned in Clifford's essay, it was clearly his central target.

There is much to recommend the idea that our beliefs should be guided by our evidence. As Clifford's tale of the ship-owner illustrates, beliefs have consequences, and those who fail to take into account the full range of evidence that is available to them may be guilty of negligence. But does that mean that we should embrace 'Clifford's dictum'—the claim that it is 'wrong always, everywhere, and for anyone, to believe anything upon insufficient evidence'? And if so, does that mean that those who believe in God violate their duties as rational agents?

Let us begin with the notion of 'sufficient evidence'. Unless we can provide a reasonable analysis of 'sufficient evidence' we won't be able to evaluate Clifford's dictum. Unfortunately, providing any such analysis is far from straightforward. One conception of sufficient evidence equates it with 'eyewitness testimony'—the kind of evidence that one has gathered oneself and which one takes to establish the truth of the relevant claim. Clifford's dictum is surely implausible if understood in these terms, for many scientific, historical, and geographical claims lie beyond our capacity to evaluate. I believe that whales and hippos have a common ancestor, that the US Civil War ended in 1865, and that the Nile is the longest river in the world, but I have not verified any one of these claims. Instead, I believe these propositions—and a great many more like them—on the basis of testimony and the authority of experts.

A more plausible conception of sufficient evidence identifies it with what is accepted by appropriately positioned individuals—'experts', in a word. Understood this way, Clifford's dictum would preserve our right to believe scientific, historical, and geographical truths of the kind considered earlier. However, as the philosopher Peter van Inwagen has pointed out, this version of Clifford's dictum runs into trouble in domains in which there are few acknowledged experts—or at least, domains in which putative experts fail to agree (which amounts to pretty much the same thing). Consider any contested claim in ethics, politics, or philosophy, such as the claim that euthanasia should be decriminalized; that free-market capitalism is conducive to human flourishing; or that consciousness is a brain process. None of these claims commands general assent among those who have reflected on them. So, if 'sufficient evidence' is equated with evidence that puts a matter beyond reasonable doubt, then Clifford's dictum would be at odds with our right to believe a great many of the ethical, political, and philosophical propositions that we do in fact believe. But this result is untenable. Worse, Clifford's dictum is surely self-undermining, for there is no consensus among reasonable persons as to whether *it* should be accepted. Proof beyond reasonable doubt is a laudable goal, but to insist that it is permissible to believe only those claims that meet this standard is to set the bar too high.

Where does this leave us with respect to the implications of divine hiddenness for the ethics of belief? As I see it, in order to show that theism is ethically suspect one would need to show that it is clearly less reasonable than belief in the kinds of claims that are the focus of ethical, political, and philosophical disagreement. Can such a case be made? Perhaps. But my own view is that it hasn't yet been made, and I see no reason to suppose that it can be made.

James on religious belief

William James (1842–1910) provided what many regard as an attractive alternative to Clifford's conception of the ethics of belief. James pointed out that we have two aims when it comes to belief: not only do we want to avoid error, we also want to obtain the truth. Clifford focused on the first of these aims, and overlooked our interest in acquiring true beliefs. James compares Clifford's attitude to that of a general who keeps his soldiers out of battle rather than risk a single wound.

> Our errors are surely not so awfully solemn things. In a world where we are so certain to incur them in spite of all our caution, a certain lightness of heart seems healthier than this excessive nervousness on their behalf.

Not only did James provide a diagnosis of where Clifford's account of belief went wrong, he also provided a provocative alternative to it. James argued that there are certain conditions in which it is legitimate for belief to outrun evidence, and for one's emotional responses—the 'passions', as James referred to them—to play a role in the fixation of belief. First, the proposition in question must be a 'live' one. In other words, it must recommend itself to the person as a serious candidate for the truth. Second, the proposition must be 'momentous'—it must matter. Third, it must be a 'forced option'—there must be no genuine possibility of suspending belief on the matter in question. When these conditions are met, James argues, it is entirely appropriate for a person's beliefs to outrun their evidence. Furthermore, he argues that these three conditions often are met in religious contexts, for religious questions are typically live, momentous, and forced. We cannot, he says, escape them by remaining sceptical, for 'although we do avoid error in that way if religion be untrue, we lose the good if it be true, just as certainly as if we positively chose to disbelieve.'

James conceived of belief as a voluntary matter—indeed, the essay in which his account appears is entitled 'The Will to Believe'—but it is possible to embrace much of what he says without committing oneself to that view. Instead of taking James to provide an account of when it is permissible to *believe* in God's existence, one could instead read him as giving an account of when it is appropriate to *accept* that God exists. What is the difference between belief and acceptance? Roughly speaking, belief in a proposition involves a categorical endorsement of its truth, whereas accepting it involves only a willingness to assume its truth for certain purposes. A scientist might accept a hypothesis about the cause of a disease for the purposes of conducting an experiment; a detective might accept a hypothesis about the identity of a murderer for the purposes of conducting her enquiries. Perhaps neither the scientist nor the detective would claim to believe their respective hypotheses, but they do use these hypotheses to guide their actions. The picture of faith that James paints for us involves a certain tentativeness. Just as the scientist is aware that his hypothesis might be false and the detective realizes that her suspect might turn out to be innocent, so too

James's person of faith proceeds on that understanding that her religious attitudes might turn out to be misguided.

This conception of faith resonates with some, but others argue that it fails to do justice to distinctive features of religious faith. In fact, there are two points at which James's conception of faith has been subject to criticism.

Some argue that James's conception of faith overlooks the emotional and existential dimensions of religious faith. Those who defend this position often appeal to the writings of the Danish philosopher Søren Kierkegaard (1813–55). Kierkegaard agrees with James that religious belief is rarely produced by argument alone, but he goes further than James does in emphasizing the role that passion plays—or at least *ought* to play—in religious life. Kierkegaard objected to the idea that religious belief should be based on an objective weighing of the evidence, for it is 'precisely in objective analysis that one loses the infinite personal and passionate concern that is the requisite condition for faith'. Religious faith, Kierkegaard argues, must involve risk and what he called 'the passion of inwardness':

> Faith is precisely the contradiction between the infinite passion of the individual's inwardness and the objective uncertainty. If I am capable of grasping God objectively, I do not believe, but precisely because I cannot do this I must believe. If I wish to preserve myself in faith I must constantly be intent upon holding fast the objective uncertainty, so as to remain out upon the deep, over seventy thousand fathoms of water, still preserving my faith.

A very different objection to James's view is that it fails to do justice to the certainty that is required for genuine religious faith. Consider again the passage from Aquinas discussed earlier, in which Aquinas contrasts faith with opinion. Opinion, says Aquinas, involves 'doubt and fear of the opposite side', whereas faith involves 'certainty and no fear of the other side'. Those who share Aquinas's conception of faith as involving a sure and firm commitment to the truth of certain propositions have reason to distance themselves from James's account.

What should we make of these two lines of criticism? Kierkegaard is certainly right to note that there is a tension between the disinterested weighing of evidence and passionate commitment. At the same time, one might argue that where evidence is altogether neglected then faith is no longer laudable but becomes a matter of irrationality, superstition, and gullibility. Aquinas, for his part, is surely right to emphasize the centrality of certainty and resoluteness to the life of faith, but one might ask whether these attitudes are appropriate given the ambiguity that surrounds religious issues. Sure and unshakeable conviction may be warranted when the case for a claim is overwhelming, but one might argue that James's attitude of 'tentative venture' is more appropriate when the evidence is patchy—as it seems to be with respect to matters theological.

Chapter 5
The problem of evil

Epicurus's challenge

In *The Brothers Karamazov*, Fyodor Dostoevsky tells the story of an 8-year-old boy who accidently wounds a general's hunting dog. In retaliation, the general orders his hounds to tear the boy to pieces in the presence of his mother. Similar examples of suffering and affliction—'evil', as the term is employed in the philosophy of religion—can be multiplied without apparent limit. From the atrocities of Hitler's Germany to the killing fields of Cambodia, from the gangland wars of Mexico to the torture-chambers of Syria, no student of history can be unaware of the horrors that human beings have inflicted on each other.

Evil poses a number of challenges for the theist. One challenge is existential. How might the theist find meaning in the face of God's apparent indifference to pain and suffering? But the challenge that is of interest to us here is theoretical rather than existential. The philosophical problem of evil is whether pain, suffering, and affliction can be reconciled with the very *existence* of God. The ancient Greek philosopher Epicurus (341–270 BCE) provided a pithy formulation of the problem:

> Is God willing to prevent evil, but not able? Then he is not omnipotent. Is he able, but not willing? Then he is malevolent. Is he both able

and willing? Whence then is evil? Is he neither able nor willing?
Then why call him God?

Philosophers of religion typically distinguish between two versions
of 'the' problem of evil: the *logical* problem of evil and the
evidential problem of evil. Roughly speaking, advocates of the
logical problem of evil regard 'evil exists' as logically inconsistent
with the proposition 'God exists'. This version of the problem of
evil provides one of the strongest challenges to theism, for it
purports to show that those who recognize the existence of evil
must deny that God exists on pain of holding inconsistent
beliefs. The evidential problem of evil is less ambitious, but no
less serious for that. Evidential arguments from evil do not
attempt to show that 'evil exists' is logically incompatible with
'God exists', but instead attempt to show only that evil—or at
least certain types of evil—provides significant evidence against
God's existence.

In response to the problem(s) of evil some theists reject the
traditional conception of God. They either conceive of God as
indifferent to suffering (and thus unwilling to prevent evil), or
they conceive of God as limited in power and/or knowledge
(and thus unable to prevent evil). Although this response to the
problem of evil does effectively undermine Epicurus's challenge,
relatively few theists have been tempted by it, for most theists
regard the commitment to God's perfect goodness, power, and
knowledge as a non-negotiable dimension of faith.

Other theists respond to the problem(s) of evil with silence. To
speculate on God's reasons for allowing evil, they argue, would be
to implicitly legitimize it, and thus exacerbate the very injustice
that prompts Epicurus's challenge in the first place. Rather than
asking how the horrors of torture, slavery, and genocide might be
justified—they continue—theists should instead condemn such
atrocities and stand in solidarity with their victims. Anything less
would be a betrayal of the very values that theists espouse.

This chapter will set these two responses to the problem(s) of evil to one side, and focus instead on those theists who think that it is possible to provide a substantive response to Epicurus's challenge without modifying the classical theistic conception of God. We can distinguish two contrasting approaches within this literature. Some theists restrict themselves to offering reasons that might, for all we know, explain why God allows evil. Accounts of this kind are known as *defences*. Other theorists offer an account of what they take God's actual reasons for allowing evil to be. Such accounts are known as *theodicies*. Note that one and the same reason can be presented in the context of either a defence or a theodicy.

Whether they are developed as defences or theodicies, almost all responses to the problem of evil involve an appeal to the 'greater good strategy'. The idea here is an intuitive one. Consider a painful medical procedure, such as a root canal. Although a root canal involves significant amounts of pain, that pain is justified insofar as the benefits that it secures both outweigh it and they couldn't have been brought about without incurring at least as much pain. We can describe the evil (pain, suffering) that accompanies the root canal as having been 'absorbed' by those benefits. Instances of evil (pain, suffering) that are not absorbed by some greater good can be described as 'unabsorbed'. Insofar as they deploy the greater good strategy, theists attempt to motivate the claim that all evils are absorbed by some good or another, and the fact that certain evils appear to be unabsorbed can be explained away.

Let us now consider some of the more influential versions of the greater good strategy.

Soul-making

One venerable version of the greater good response suggests that evil might be justified by the possibilities that it provides for moral development and growth. A world without suffering—it is claimed—would be a world without compassion, patience, tolerance, or forgiveness. These goods are known as second-order goods, for their exercise requires the presence of first-order evils. Compassion is possible only in the presence of suffering; forgiveness is possible only when one has been wronged; and heroism is possible only where danger is a real possibility. A world without evil would contain no opportunities for character development, for it would be devoid of compassion, forgiveness, and heroism. This response to the problem of evil has its roots in the writings of the 2nd-century writer St Irenaeus, and was influentially defended in the 20th century by the British theologian John Hick (1922–2012).

One challenge to the soul-making response concerns the fragile connection between the evils of the world and soul-making. Suffering certainly *can* act as a catalyst for moral development, but it can also embitter. Elie Wiesel's *Night* recounts his experiences in the concentration camps of Auschwitz and Buchenwald, and his subsequent alienation and disgust with humanity (see Figure 6).

Even when pain and suffering do prompt the development of character and the exercise of virtue, it is a further question whether these goods absorb the evils that give rise to them. A second-order good does not necessarily absorb the first-order evils that occasion it. You cannot forgive me unless I have insulted you, but the goodness that is associated with your forgiveness does not justify the badness of my insult, and it would have been better if I hadn't insulted you in the first place. Indeed, the assumption—implicit in the soul-making theodicy—that the goods associated with virtue and character development absorb the evils that occasion them has a number of implausible consequences. If God allows syphilis, starvation, and solitary confinement because of the opportunities that they provide for moral development, then perhaps our attempts to eradicate these phenomena are misguided. Perhaps we should no longer vaccinate children against typhoid, rubella, and rabies, but instead welcome these

6. Felix Nussbaum's 'Camp Synagogue at Saint Cyprien'.

diseases as providing opportunities for character-building. These suggestions are surely perverse, but it is unclear what grounds the advocate of the soul-making theodicy has for rejecting them.

Even if advocates of the soul-making theodicy can show that the benefits of soul-making are absorbed by the badness of the evils that give rise to them, one might ask why soul-making is necessary in the first place. Perhaps *we* must be exposed to pain and suffering in order to become virtuous moral agents, but why didn't God create creatures who were innately disposed to display moral virtue—creatures that don't require the kind of moral training that we do?

A final challenge facing the soul-making theodicy concerns its ability to explain the suffering of creatures who lack the capacity for moral development. What might non-human animals and very young children who have been subjected to cruel and degrading treatment learn from their suffering? Rather than functioning as opportunities for character development, such experiences often serve only to make animals and young children fearful and aggressive. So even if an appeal to soul-making could justify the suffering of self-conscious creatures like ourselves, it is difficult to see how it could justify the suffering of animals and young children.

Laws of nature

A second greater good response—the natural law response—is explicitly designed to address the challenge posed by 'natural evils'. Natural evils are evils that are caused by natural phenomena, such as death, disease, and natural disasters, as opposed to the evils that are caused by the deliberate actions of agents (which are known as 'moral evils').

At the heart of the natural law response is the assumption that natural evils are a necessary consequence of having laws of nature, and without laws of nature meaningful moral agency would be impossible. Laws of nature are needed for meaningful moral agency, because meaningful moral agency requires knowledge of the consequences of our actions, and it is only if we have the capacity for meaningful moral agency that we have true responsibility—which is in and of itself a great good.

The natural law response is open to many challenges. One challenge concerns the assumption that natural evils—death, disease, and natural disasters—are a necessary consequence of the existence of laws of nature. Could a world without death, disease, and natural disasters not be law-governed? More generally, could we not have acquired the knowledge needed for moral agency without having actually encountered natural evils? After all, theists presumably take God to have had this knowledge independently of the existence of natural evil, which would indicate that the existence of natural evil isn't logically required for the possession of this knowledge.

Even if it is granted that the knowledge needed for moral agency requires the existence of some natural evils, it is a further question whether acquiring that knowledge requires either the amount of natural evil that the world contains or the kinds of natural evil that it contains. Surely, one might think, we could have acquired the knowledge needed for moral agency without the suffering of animals that occurred prior to the evolution of human beings, or without the violence that has characterized the history of our species.

Free will

Although both the soul-making and natural law responses have their advocates, by far the most influential response to the problem of evil is the free will response. As the label suggests, the free will response holds that evil is absorbed by the possession of free will, and that even an omnipotent being could not have provided us with free will without allowing evil—or at least the possibility thereof. This response to the problem of evil has its roots in the writings of the 4th-century African philosopher and Christian Bishop St Augustine, and was given a new lease of life in the late 20th century by the American philosopher Alvin Plantinga (1932–).

An obvious challenge to the free will response concerns its ability to account for natural evils. On the face of things, the free will response would seem to be able to justify only the pain and suffering that results from the deliberate exercise of free will (moral evil), and it is unclear how it might account for the evil which results from natural phenomenon, such as earthquakes, volcanoes, or disease.

Although some free will theorists hold that natural evils are best dealt with by appealing to another greater good response (such as the soul-making or natural law responses), Plantinga responds to the challenge of natural evil by suggesting that for all we know natural evils are caused by immaterial agents (such as the Devil), and thus that all evil is actually 'moral evil' insofar as it results from the abuse of free will. This assumption is legitimate given that Plantinga's aim is only to show that 'God exists' and 'evil exists' are logically consistent. If, however, he had been attempting to show that evil doesn't provide evidence against God's existence, then he would need to have motivated the claim that natural evils result from the actions of free agents.

A further question raised by the free will response is whether the goods that are associated with free agency outweigh the evils to which it gives rise. It is, I think, not entirely obvious what the answer to this question is. Reflecting on the horrors that occur in the death camps and torture cells of this world, one might well wonder whether the benefits of free will are absorbed by the evils that it allows. At the same time, our willingness to bring children into this world suggests that we regard human existence as fundamentally good, despite the pain and suffering to which we are all vulnerable.

Most discussion of the free will response has focused not on whether the goods associated with free will absorb the evils of the world, but whether it would have been possible for an omnipotent being to have secured those goods without allowing evil to exist. (Remember that if a good could have been secured without the corresponding evil then it fails to 'absorb' that evil.) We might call this *Mackie's challenge*, in honour of the philosopher J.L. Mackie, who articulated it with vividness:

> [I]f God has made men such that in their free choices they sometimes prefer what is good and sometimes what is evil, why could he not have made men such that they always freely choose the good? If there is no logical impossibility in a man's freely choosing the good on one, or on several, occasions, there cannot be a logical impossibility in his freely choosing the good on every occasion. God was not, then, faced with a choice between making innocent

automata and making beings who, in acting freely, would sometimes go wrong: there was open to him the obviously better possibility of making beings who would act freely but always go right. Clearly, his failure to avail himself of this possibility is inconsistent with his being both omnipotent and wholly good.

Mackie's challenge raises many deep and difficult issues, and we can here only scratch the surface of the huge literature that it has generated.

The first issue concerns the analysis of free will, and the debate between compatibilists and incompatibilists. Incompatibilists claim that free will and determinism are not compatible, whereas compatibilists claim that they are. (Determinism is the claim that the initial state of the world together with the laws of nature jointly necessitate all of its future states.) The debate between compatibilists and incompatibilists bears on the evaluation of Mackie's challenge, for if free will is possible in a deterministic world, then God could have created agents who always freely choose the good simply by creating a world with initial conditions and laws of nature which necessitate only good states of affairs. In short, the free will response succeeds only if an incompatibilist account of free will is assumed.

Few theists will regard this fact as problematic, for theists typically are incompatibilists. However, some philosophers think that compatibilism provides the only viable approach to free will. Theorists of this stripe will regard the fact that the free will response presupposes incompatibilism as a serious liability for it.

Even assuming incompatibilism, one might ask why God couldn't have created free agents who always choose good over evil. As Mackie notes, there doesn't seem to be anything *incoherent* in the idea of a created being who is both perfectly free and perfectly good. And if the concept of such an agent is coherent, then it seems to follow that an omnipotent God could have created such agents.

In response to this challenge, some argue that God wasn't in a position to distinguish morally perfect agents from agents who would abuse their free will. According to this view, God took a risk in creating free agents, and didn't know whether or not the agents that had been created would abuse their free will. Although this version of the free will response succeeds in blocking Mackie's challenge, many theists find it deeply unappealing, for it represents God as a gambler—a creator who in some deep sense didn't know how things would turn out.

Plantinga offers a very different response to Mackie's challenge. Mackie assumes that because there is no logical incoherence in the idea of a free, but morally perfect, creature, it follows that it must have been possible for God to bring such creatures into existence. Plantinga challenges this assumption, arguing that for all we know an omnipotent God might have lacked this ability. Plantinga develops this proposal by appealing to the notion of a creaturely essence, where a creature's essence specifies what that creature will do in every possible situation in which it finds itself. He argues it is possible that the only essences that God could instantiate (that is, the only beings that God could have created) have the peculiar property of being such that the relevant creature performs at least one morally wrong action.

A full evaluation of Plantinga's proposal would require examining his notion of a creaturely essence and his conception of necessity, and these are not topics that we can broach here. Suffice it to say, however, that although the details of his account continue to attract discussion, many philosophers regard Plantinga as having shown that there may be logically possible states of affairs that even an omnipotent God can't bring about. Does that mean that Plantinga has solved the problem of evil? Not at all. Plantinga aimed only to address Mackie's logical problem of evil, and to show that 'God exists' and 'evil exists' are logically consistent. Even if he succeeded in that regard, evil might nonetheless provide robust evidence against the existence of God.

Horrendous evils

One final challenge to the free will response—indeed, to all greater good responses—takes the form of what the philosopher Marilyn McCord Adams (1943–2017) has called 'horrendous evils'. Adams gives as examples of such evils the rape of a woman and the axing off of her arms, psycho-physical torture whose ultimate goal is the disintegration of personality, and slow death by starvation. In each case the evil that the person has suffered threatens to overwhelm her life and render it meaningless.

Adams goes on to argue that the standard theistic responses to the problem of evil lack the resources to engage with horrendous evils. This is because the standard responses to the problem of evil assume a global conception of God's goodness, according to which God's goodness requires only that the world as a whole is good. For example, advocates of the free will response hold that the evils of the world are absorbed by the benefits that derive from the possession of free will. However, Adams points out that most theistic traditions are committed to a *creature-centred* conception of God's goodness, according to which God's goodness ensures that each creature's life is good *for that creature*. Horrendous evils pose an acute challenge to this aspect of God's goodness, for their victims have reason to doubt whether their overall life has been good for them. As Dostoevsky's character Ivan asks in the *Brothers Karamazov*, why should abused children be made to pay for the harmony of the world?

Having identified the challenge posed by horrendous evils, Adams then attempts to meet it by drawing on the value theory of her religious tradition, Christianity. She argues that only post-mortem intimacy with God—the 'beatific vision' referred to by mystics such as Julian of Norwich—would be able to defeat horrendous evils, and thus that the theist has decisive reason to think that divine intimacy of this kind obtains.

Adams is widely regarded as having identified a particularly acute version of the problem of evil. However, her proposed solution to it has had a rather more ambivalent reception. One problem is that even if the goodness of the beatific vision *outweighs* the badness of horrendous evils, it doesn't *absorb* those evils unless they are necessary for the beatific vision, and Adams does not explain why such evils might be necessary for the beatific vision (or any other good for that matter). Why—one is tempted to ask—couldn't God have created us in a state in which we already enjoy the beatific vision? A second challenge concerns the notion of the afterlife required by Adams's account, for it is far from obvious that post-mortem existence is a possibility for creatures like us (see Chapter 8). A third challenge concerns animal suffering. Non-human animals may not be able to experience the depths of abject misery to which human beings are subject, but they can surely suffer in horrific ways. In order to ensure that God is good to such animals, the theist might need to assume that they too are able to enjoy some form of post-mortem intimacy with God.

Sceptical responses

The responses to the problem of evil that we have surveyed thus far all attempt to specify goods whose existence might explain why God allows evil. (As we have noted, defences treat these goods as accounts of why God *might* allow evil, whereas theodicies treat them as accounts of why God actually *does* allow evil.)

A very different approach to the problem of evil makes no attempt to specify the goods that absorb evil, but instead aims only to make plausible the idea that we can't tell whether or not the evils of the world are absorbed. Sceptical theists, as the advocates of this position are known, hold that our cognitive limitations prevent us from being able to reliably discriminate absorbed evils from unabsorbed evils, and thus that we have no reason to think that apparently unabsorbed evils really are unabsorbed.

The attractions of sceptical theism are perhaps best appreciated by considering the situation of a young child who requires painful medical treatment. Such a child might be unable to grasp the justification for this treatment, either because she fails to realize that the pain involved in the treatment is outweighed by the benefits that it will bring, or because she fails to understand that those benefits cannot be secured without the treatment. Sceptical theists argue that we suffer from the kinds of limitations that the child does, and that just as the child's inability to grasp the justification for the treatment provides her with no reason to think that the treatment is unjustified, so too our inability to understand why God allows evil provides us with no reason to think that God has no justification for allowing evil.

The sceptical theist is clearly committed to the idea that our ignorance lies at the heart of the problem of evil, but it is less clear what precisely they take us to be ignorant of. One possibility is that we are ignorant of the goods that absorb the evils of the world. Just as certain goods, such as the appreciation of music, lie beyond the ken of most animals, so too there may be goods that lie beyond our ken. Perhaps communion with God is such a good. A second possibility is that although we are aware of the goods that absorb apparently unabsorbed evils, we fail to appreciate their true value, and thus fail to recognize their power to absorb evils. Consider, for example, our views of empathy. Although we do regard empathy with the victims of torture as a good, we don't regard it is able to absorb the evil that is involved in the torture itself. The sceptical theist might suggest that this view is mistaken, and that from an objective or 'God's eye' point of view empathy is a great good—one that can absorb even the horror of torture. A third possibility is that although we are aware of both the states of affairs whose goodness absorbs the evils of the world, and their true value, we fail to grasp the fact that these goods cannot be realized unless certain evils obtain. On this view, we are akin to the child who knows that the pain caused by a medical procedure is outweighed by the value of saving her life, but fails to realize that unless she has the procedure she will die. These possibilities are obviously not mutually exclusive, and sceptical theist could hold that we are ignorant in all three of these ways.

What should we make of sceptical theism? It is certainly true that we are cognitively limited in many ways—that much is beyond doubt. What is less clear is whether we are cognitively limited in the ways required by sceptical theism. Further, it can be argued that taking ourselves to suffer from the kinds of cognitive limitations posited by the scepticism thesis would undermine the possibility of moral agency, for moral agency requires a grasp of the possible consequences of one's actions, their relative values, and the ways in which those consequences are related to each other.

Consider a doctor who is faced with decisions about whether or not to operate on a sick child. Making such a decision requires understanding: the likely outcome of the surgery (although the procedure will be painful, it is likely to save the child's life); the value of this outcome relative to its alternatives (the badness of the pain caused by the surgery is outweighed by the goodness of saving the child's life); and the ways in which the surgery is related to this outcome (it is likely that the child will survive if, but only if, the procedure is performed). Effective moral agency is not possible in the absence of such knowledge, as is demonstrated by the fact that young children are not effective moral agents. The sceptical theist is open to the charge that our attempts to improve the world are as misguided as a 4-year-old's attempts to run a hospital would be, and that for all we know our efforts to eradicate evil are likely to do as much harm as good. But surely no theist should be willing to deny that we can be effective moral agents. In short, the challenges that face the sceptical response to the problem of evil are no less pressing than those that confront other versions of the greater good strategy.

As we have seen, theists have offered a number of responses to the problem(s) of evil, and debate continues regarding the merits of these responses. Few, however, would deny that evil represents the most serious challenge to belief in God. It is not for nothing that the Catholic theologian Hans Küng once described the problem of evil as 'the rock of atheism'.

Chapter 6
The roots of religious belief

Homo religiosus

One of the features of human societies that would surely capture the attention of any visitor to our planet is the ubiquity of religious commitment. Unlike science, which requires rather specialized social conditions in order to flourish, religion occurs in the vast majority of societies—indeed, it can be plausibly argued that religion is a human universal. We are *Homo religiosus*—creatures who embrace religious ideas as readily as we engage in singing, dancing, and telling jokes.

Why do we find religious ideas compelling? One might be tempted to answer this question by appealing to the arguments for God's existence, such as those that we examined in Chapter 2. Whether or not these arguments *actually* provide good reasons for the existence of God (or supernatural agents more generally), perhaps religious ideas have such wide appeal because human beings take them to be persuasive.

But although arguments for God's existence are likely to explain why *some* people embrace religious ideas, it is doubtful whether they play a significant role in accounting for the general appeal of religion. In most cultures the existence of the gods (or a God) is regarded as obvious, something that hardly requires argument.

Even when people do present arguments to justify their religious convictions, these arguments often seem to be post-hoc justifications for religious belief rather than articulations of their actual psychological basis. (In this respect, arguments for God's existence resemble the arguments that philosophers give for the existence of the external world: their primary role is to convince the sceptic, rather than to describe the basis of ordinary belief in the existence of an external world.) To identify the fundamental roots of religious belief we need to look beyond the arguments for God's existence.

The standard model

Speculation on the genesis of religion is an age-old enterprise. The ancient Greek historian Diodorus Siculus suggested that the attractiveness of religious ideas derives from our fear of the unknown and our desire for environmental control.

> Fortune has never bestowed an unmixed happiness on mankind; but with all her gifts has ever conjoined some disastrous circumstance, in order to chastise men with a reverence for the gods, whom, in prosperity, they are apt to neglect and forget.

Siculus's comments have been echoed by a number of writers down the ages. David Hume claimed that religion 'arises chiefly from an anxious fear'; Sigmund Freud took religion to be 'born from man's need to make his helplessness tolerable'; and Karl Marx viewed religion as a mechanism that enables us to cope with miserable social conditions—it is, he wrote, 'the sigh of the oppressed creature'.

It is not hard to see some truth in these proposals. Many religions have gods whose role is to ensure success in uncertain ventures (such as the cultivation of crops or war), and the notion of an afterlife (a core commitment of many religions) promises to address one of our greatest fears—that of death.

But despite these points, few contemporary theorists endorse this 'wish-fulfilment' account of the roots of religion. One reason for this is that religious convictions are as often a source of fear as they are a source of solace, and for every benevolent god it is possible to find at least one that is malevolent or capricious. Indeed, even the promise of an afterlife is by no means an unmixed blessing, for although some individuals die happy in the knowledge that heaven awaits them, others go to their grave with the threat of God's punishment hanging over them. Religious ideas certainly can function as an opiate to relieve suffering in the way that Marx suggested, but there is little evidence that religion dissipates with the development of benevolent social conditions.

For these reasons, the idea that religion is grounded in the need to deal with life's contingencies generally takes a backseat in contemporary accounts of religious belief. Instead, current accounts of religious belief emphasize three other factors: the activity of a hypersensitive agency detection device; the intuitive pull of teleological explanations; and the need to ensure that the members of a society comply with its norms. Taken together, these three elements comprise what we might describe as the 'standard model' of religious belief. Let us consider each element in turn.

For much of human history, the most virulent threats facing us have been those that are posed by other agents—animals of various kinds, and in particular other human beings. Those of us who are lucky enough to enjoy the protections that are afforded by modern society rarely come face-to-face with marauding animals or rampaging members of our own species, but in earlier ages these threats would have been only too common. In order to deal with them we developed a specialized cognitive mechanism that alerts us to the presence of agents—an agency detection device. By signalling the presence of agents, this mechanism enables us to detect potential predators, prey, and sources of protection.

As the anthropologist Stewart Guthrie has pointed out, there is ample evidence that this agency detection device is 'hypersensitive': it generates an 'agent here' signal on the basis of very little evidence. Suppose that you are camping in the woods and hear mysterious sounds at night. Your first thought is likely to be that the sounds are caused by a predator of some kind, and only later might you realize that they were caused by the wind in the trees. Having a hypersensitive agency detection device makes good sense from an evolutionary point of view, for false positives (e.g. mistaking the wind for a predator) are likely to lead to nothing worse than a sleepless night, whereas false negatives (e.g. mistaking a predator for the wind) can be fatal.

The robustness of our tendency to perceive intentional agency is illustrated by a study conducted by the psychologists Fritz Heider and Marianne Simmel in the 1940s. Participants were shown a short film in which a number of two-dimensional figures (e.g. two triangles and a rectangle) moved in ways that were suggestive of agency. These figures were clearly nothing more than geometrical shapes, but the participants found it natural to view them as intentional agents. For example, they described the big triangle as 'chasing' the little triangle; the little triangle as 'fleeing' from the big one; and the rectangle as 'sheltering' the little triangle.

Although our agency detector uses physical cues to detect the presence of (putative) agents, we find it natural to conceive of agents themselves in immaterial terms. In the words of the American psychologist Paul Bloom, we are *intuitive dualists*. From Homer's *Odyssey*, in which Circe changes men to pigs, to *Shrek 2*, in which an ogre is transformed into a human being, literature is replete with stories of agents migrating from one body to another—or indeed, existing in a disembodied state. Religions, of course, capitalize on our intuitive dualism, for the typical religious universe is populated with immaterial agents of various kinds—gods, demons, angels, and ancestors.

The second component of the standard account concerns the appeal of teleological explanations—that is, explanations that invoke the aims of agents (as opposed to those that invoke physical or evolutionary causes). We find teleological explanations intuitively compelling—they 'feel right' to us. Consider the widespread tendency to explain mysterious natural phenomena by reference to the actions of supernatural agents. For example, the ancient Greeks took Zeus to be responsible for thunder and lightning, while the ancient Japanese believed that earthquakes are caused by a catfish called Namazu (see Figure 7).

Psychologists have found that a predilection for teleological explanations is in place from a very early age. In one study, preschoolers and adults were asked what they thought living things, artifacts, and non-living natural objects were 'for', while explicitly being given the option of saying they were not 'for' anything. The adults assigned functions only to certain things (such as clocks and pockets), whereas the preschoolers assigned functions indiscriminately, claiming not only that clocks and pockets have functions, but so too do mountains ('for climbing'), clouds ('for raining'), babies ('for loving'), and animals ('for walking around'). Another study asked adults and a group of 7- and 8-years-olds to choose between two explanations for why a collection of rocks were pointy: a process-based explanation (e.g. 'bits of stuff piled up for a long period of time') and a teleological explanation (e.g. 'so that animals could scratch on them when they got itchy'). The adults preferred the process-based explanation, whereas the 7- and 8-year-olds preferred the teleological explanation. As Deborah Kelemen, the author of these studies, put it, children appear to be 'promiscuous teleologists'.

The third component of the standard account of religious belief concerns the problem of norm compliance. The starting point of this problem begins with the importance of norms for the success of social groups. For example, a group might have the norm that any individual who has secured a supply of food should share it

7. Namazu.

with the rest of the community. Groups whose members comply with norms of this kind will have a competitive advantage over groups that lack such a norm (or in which it is routinely flouted). However, it is difficult for groups to secure compliance with its norms. It's in your interest for me to share any food that I have found, but it's in my interest to keep that food to myself. How then can groups ensure that their members comply with their norms, given that each member has self-interested reasons to flout them?

In the modern world the problem of norm compliance is solved by a mix of moral education and the threat of community-sanctioned force. These mechanisms also exist in traditional societies, but they are often supplemented by a third—and potentially more powerful—source of norm compliance: the threat of supernatural punishment. One of the central functions that are assigned to God is that of ensuring that the wicked are punished. And God, of course, is in a much better position to perform this function than human beings are. We have imperfect knowledge of our neighbours' deeds, but God is omniscient. We may be (seen to be) biased in judging our neighbours' motivations, but God is perfectly just. We may be afraid to censure our neighbours for fear of retaliation, but God has no such fear. (Moreover, divine omnipotence ensures that the wicked will be punished—if not in this life then surely in the next.) Religion frees a community from needing to police its own members by out-sourcing the job to supernatural agents.

The idea that moral transgression will incur the wrath of supernatural agents is not limited to small-scale pre-industrial societies, but can be found in the work of many Enlightenment thinkers. John Locke claimed that bonds of human society 'can have no hold upon or sanctity for an atheist; for the taking away of God, even only in thought, dissolves all'. Dostoevsky put a rather more pithy formulation of the same point into the mouth of his character Ivan Karamazov: 'without God everything is permitted'. Whether or not the rejection of God does indeed entail moral nihilism is irrelevant here. The point, rather, is that belief in the existence of supernatural agents who reward virtue and punish vice is psychologically motivating, and groups in which this belief is assumed will have an advantage over those in which it isn't.

Implications of the standard model

Although the standard model continues to be the subject of debate, let us assume that it—or at least something very much like it—is true. What implications might it have for the rationality of religious belief?

Many theorists claim that the standard model not only explains religion but that it also explains it *away*. Let us call such theorists 'sceptics'. To use a term that we owe to the Oxford philosopher Peter Kail, sceptics regard the standard model as constituting a *destabilizing path* to belief, where a path to belief is destabilizing if knowledge about it provides one with a reason to think that the belief is false. Destabilizing paths to belief can be contrasted with two other paths to belief: *vindicatory* paths and *neutral* paths. A path to belief is vindicatory if knowledge about it provides one with a reason to think that the belief is true, and it is neutral if it is neither destabilizing nor vindicatory. It will be useful to have a label for the claim that the standard model constitutes a destabilizing path to belief. Let us call this the *destabilizing thesis*.

There is a long tradition of regarding scientific accounts of religious belief—what Hume called 'natural histories of religion'—as destabilizing paths to belief. Indeed, Hume viewed his own account of the genesis of religious belief in this light. But Hume's natural history of religion differs from the standard model, and even if Hume was right to regard his account as undermining the reasonableness of religious belief, it is a further question whether the standard model does likewise. How might the destabilizing thesis be defended?

The by-product argument

One argument for the destabilizing thesis appeals to the idea that if the standard model is true, then religious beliefs are the incidental by-products of mechanisms that have been selected by evolution to serve other purposes. Consider, for example, the hypersensitive agency detector. The sceptic will argue that the hypersensitive agency detector evolved so that we could detect terrestrial agents—predators, prey, and potential protectors. It didn't evolve so that we might detect angels, demons, or gods. But—the argument continues—religious beliefs are unlikely to be true if they are the incidental by-products of the mechanisms that generate them.

There are two ways in which one might respond to this argument. First, one might take issue with the assumption that religious beliefs *are* incidental by-products of the cognitive mechanisms that produce them. Theists hold that our cognitive mechanisms were designed by God. Thus, they are likely to argue that the agency detector was designed to enable us to detect both natural and supernatural agents. Similarly, the theist will argue that our predilection for teleological explanations is perfectly in line with our design plan: our cognitive faculties were fashioned in this manner so that we might find it natural to think that God created the world. To assume that religious beliefs are the incidental by-products of mechanisms that have been selected for other purposes seems to beg the question against theism.

A second response to the by-product argument rejects the assumption that being the by-product of a cognitive mechanism undermines a belief's credentials. Consider beliefs about highly theoretical domains, such as polymer chemistry, quantitative easing, or black holes. Evolution did not sculpt our minds so that we might gain insight into these highly theoretical fields. Rather, our cognitive capacities were shaped so that we might solve rather more mundane problems, such as those associated with avoiding predators, finding prey, and identifying possible sexual partners. So if the by-product argument were sound then it would follow that our beliefs about polymer chemistry, quantitative easing, and black holes are unjustified. But surely that would be the wrong result. Indeed, the by-product argument seems to be self-undermining, for belief in the standard model is itself surely a by-product of the cognitive mechanisms that generate it.

The argument from explanatory absence

A second argument for the destabilizing thesis focuses on the idea that if the standard account is right, then God plays no role in explaining why people have religious beliefs. Instead, the existence of religious belief can be explained by appeal to purely natural mechanisms, such as hypersensitive agency detectors. But if an explanation for why people believe that God exists is itself silent on God's existence, then—the argument runs—the warrant for such beliefs is thereby undermined. Call this the argument from *explanatory absence*.

To appreciate where this argument might be vulnerable consider the following scenario. Suppose that I believe that there is an alpaca on my lawn. You might explain why I hold this belief by appealing to certain types of activity in my brain. This neurological explanation (which, we can suppose, is correct) fails to mention the alpaca that I take myself to see, or indeed any alpacas at all. In other words, the alpaca is absent from the explanation that you provide for my belief in its existence. Thus, if God's absence from the standard model undermines religious belief, then the alpaca's absence from the explanation of my alpaca belief should also undermine it. But surely that would be the wrong result, for the neural explanation of my alpaca belief clearly *doesn't* undermine it. Thus, there must be something wrong with the argument from explanatory absence—at least as it is presented here.

We can see where the argument goes wrong by distinguishing a *partial* explanation of a belief from a *full* explanation of it. The neural explanation of my alpaca belief is merely partial, for it mentions only the immediate causes of my belief. A complete explanation of my belief would need to include the causes of my neural activity, and in most cases such an explanation *would* involve the alpaca. Indeed, if the alpaca doesn't feature as an element in the full explanation of my belief (because, for example, my belief that there is an alpaca on my lawn is caused by a hallucination), then the path to my alpaca belief is likely to have been exposed as destabilizing and thus the warrant for it will have been undermined.

How do these points bear on the question of religious belief? The sceptic assumes that the standard model provides a full explanation of religious belief. The theist, however, will argue that at best the standard model provides only a partial explanation of religious belief. In other words, the theist might accept that the standard model is true, but she will argue that it doesn't represent the *whole* truth. As the theist sees things, the mechanisms of belief-formation described by the standard model exist only because of God's creative activity, and thus a complete explanation of religious belief will invoke God.

Of course, the sceptic is unlikely to be persuaded by this response, for she will argue that as far as cognitive science is concerned there is no need to appeal to God. Adding God to the standard model would be unmotivated: God would be a wheel that turned for no purpose. But the theist might not be interested in persuading the sceptic that God must be added to the standard model. The theist might be interested only in whether the truth of the standard model undermines theism given everything else that she accepts. And arguably it doesn't, for the theist can treat the standard model as a description of the mechanisms underlying our natural religious inclinations—mechanisms that she ascribes to God's creative activity.

The argument from unreliability

A third argument for the destabilizing thesis focuses on the apparent unreliability of the mechanisms described by the standard model. Let us briefly review these mechanisms, with an eye to the question of their reliability.

Consider first the hyperactive agency detector device. As we have already noted, this device is so-called because of its tendency to generate false positives. It can be likened to a fire alarm that goes off at the slightest provocation. Thus, the sceptic will argue that if a hyperactive agency detector lies at the root of religious belief, then those beliefs are unlikely to be true. Similar considerations apply to the second strand of the standard model—our predilection for teleological explanations. The sceptic will argue that just as we go wrong when we explain the pointiness of rocks in terms of an animal's need to scratch itself, so too we go wrong in taking lightning to be caused by Zeus's anger. We have a general tendency to explain non-teleological phenomena in teleological terms. What about the third strand of the standard model, which explains the existence of religious belief in terms of its role in ensuring that individuals conform to the norms of their group? Here, too, the sceptic would appear to be on solid ground, for the success of this account does require that there *are* supernatural agents who will punish defectors. Instead, all that matters is that societies in which the existence of such agents is assumed will have a competitive advantage of those in which it isn't. The general picture that emerges from the foregoing is one on which although religious beliefs might be true, their truth would be purely accidental. They might be likened to the beliefs that are acquired by consulting a broken clock. Beliefs formed in this way will occasionally be right, but knowing how they are formed surely provides one with a reason to doubt their truth.

Although this is perhaps the strongest argument for the destabilizing thesis, it too can be challenged. To see how, consider whether vision is a reliable basis on which to form beliefs. As posed, it is unclear whether this question has a determinate answer, for there are contexts in which vision is reliable and others in which it isn't. Other things being equal, looking at medium-sized objects that are appropriately illuminated is likely to lead to accurate beliefs about them, whereas looking at objects that are extremely small or poorly illuminated is generally an unreliable way of forming beliefs about them. With this point in mind, the theist might argue that even if the mechanisms that generate religious beliefs are often unreliable, they may be reliable in those contexts in which they give rise to religious beliefs. After all, these mechanisms sometimes deliver trustworthy beliefs. Footsteps outside one's door typically indicate the presence of visitors, and the marks that we have discovered on the walls of the Lascaux caves were surely the products of intentional design. To assume that the mechanisms invoked by the standard model are unreliable in specifically religious contexts begs the question against theism.

An important lesson has emerged from the preceding discussion: the plausibility of the destabilizing thesis depends on the perspective that one adopts. From the perspective of someone without religious commitments the standard model does indeed appear to treat religion as resting on a destabilizing path to belief, for it suggests that religious belief can be accounted for without positing the existence of God (the argument from explanatory absence) and that the mechanisms implicated in religious belief are unreliable (the argument from unreliability). However, neither of these arguments is compelling from the theist's perspective, for the theist holds that God has designed us to find religious ideas intuitively compelling. It is unclear whether there is independent reason to favour one of these positions over the other—independent, that is, of taking a stance on the very question that divides theists from non-theists. To paraphrase the philosopher T.J. Mawson (who was himself paraphrasing St Augustine), non-theists might be justified in thinking that our brains have 'made God' for themselves, whereas theists might be justified in thinking that God has made us our brains for Godself.

Chapter 7
Speaking of God

Realism and anti-realism

Language plays many roles in religious thought and practice. It is used in prayer to communicate with God; it is used in sermons to instruct and encourage the members of religious communities; and it is used in religious texts to describe historical events and to articulate moral prescriptions. Philosophers of religion, however, are most interested in the doctrinal uses of language. Consider, for example, the opening words of the Christian Church's Nicene Creed: 'We believe in one God, the Father Almighty, Maker of heaven and earth, and of all things visible and invisible.' Consider also the Islamic Shahada: 'There is no god but Allah and Muhammad is his messenger.' Or consider the Mahāvākya (Grand Pronouncement) from the *Chandogya Upanishad*, 'Tat tvam asi', which is typically interpreted to mean that the self is identical to Ultimate Reality. On the face of things, these claims are truth-evaluable assertions: descriptions of reality that are either true or false. As such, they seem to have the same function as many of the claims made in science and everyday life, such as 'Volcanoes are caused by seismic activity' or 'Inflation is rising'. Of course, it might be more difficult to tell whether religious claims are true than it is to tell whether everyday or even scientific claims are true, but—it seems plausible to suppose—the claims themselves are relatively straightforward: they are attempts to describe reality.

The conception of religious language just outlined is referred to as realism. Although realism is widely endorsed, some theorists reject realism in favour of an anti-realist conception of religious language. Anti-realists grant that religious utterances *seem* to be attempts to describe reality, but they argue that this appearance is misleading, and that religious language actually serves a very different linguistic function. One of the most influential versions of anti-realism construes religious utterances as expressions of emotional states or attitudes. Rather than being understood on the model of 'Volcanoes are caused by seismic activity' or 'Inflation is rising', anti-realists of this stripe hold that 'God exists' should be understood on the model of 'Wow!' or 'Yippeee!'—it expresses a certain attitude to life. As D.Z. Phillips, an influential proponent of this view, puts it: '"God exists" is not a statement of fact. You might say that it is not in the indicative mood. "There is a God," though it appears to be in the indicative mood, is an expression of faith.'

One motivation for anti-realism derives from the verificationist theory of meaning, according to which a statement can have the function of describing reality only if it is possible to verify (or, on other versions of the view, falsify) it. The verificationist theory of meaning has been taken to cast doubt on the meaningfulness of religious claims, for it is not clear that religious assertions are verifiable. We know how to verify the claim that inflation is rising, but—the worry goes—we don't know how to verify typical religious claims, such as 'God exists'. God is supposed to be transcendent, and thus outside the realm of what is amenable to observation and experiment. But if God's existence is not verifiable, and if being verifiable is a condition on being meaningful, then 'God exists' cannot be meaningful. And if 'God exists' isn't meaningful then utterances of this statement do not constitute descriptions of the world but must have some other function. For example, they might be expressions of the believer's values and commitments.

Although the line of argument just sketched was once influential, it has few contemporary advocates for the verificationist theory of meaning has been discredited. There are a number of reasons for this, but perhaps the most powerful objection to verificationism is that there are many obviously meaningful claims for which verification conditions proved extremely difficult to specify. Indeed, verificationism appears to dissolve in its own acids (as the theologian Janet Soskice once put it), for it is not easy to specify verification conditions for the theory itself. How would one go about verifying the claim that a sentence is meaningful only if it is possible to verify it?

Let us leave verificationism to one side and consider the inherent plausibility of anti-realism. Is religious language only ever used to express emotional states and attitudes? Surely not. It is obviously *possible* to use religious language without meaning to make truth-evaluable claims—one might, for example, recite the Nicene creed simply because one wishes to identify with one's community—but it is implausible to suppose that religious language is never used to make truth-evaluable claims. Moreover, even when religious utterances are used to express one's emotional attitudes, such uses often presuppose that they have truth-evaluable content. The theist who asserts that the world was created by God might indeed be meaning to express his attitude of hope and optimism, but that attitude will typically be grounded in the belief that the world was indeed made by God. Should that belief turn out to be false then that hope will have been unmasked as ill-founded. The philosopher Roger Trigg seems to me to get things exactly right: 'Religions are typically making claims about the nature of reality, and pretending that they are something quite different is to misrepresent their nature.'

The names of God

In Arthur C. Clarke's short story 'The Nine Billion Names of God', the monks of a Tibetan monastery use a computer to compile a complete list of the names of God, and in so doing usher in the end of the world. Clarke's story captures something of the awe and mystery that has often accompanied the act of naming God. Perhaps it is for this reason that many religions have prohibitions on speaking or writing God's name, and instead use codes and ciphers to refer to the divine.

For the philosopher, the names of God are also a source of wonder and fascination. How, if at all, could a name succeed in referring to divine reality? Could terms that are associated with different religious traditions—'Yahweh', 'God', and 'Allah', for example—refer to the same divine reality, so that Jews, Christians, and Muslims all worship the same being, or should we assume that 'Yahweh', 'God', and 'Allah' refer to different beings (if indeed they refer at all)? In addition to their obvious philosophical interest, these questions also have political implications. In 2014, the Malaysian high court ruled that the Catholic church was no longer permitted to use the word 'Allah', presumably on the grounds that 'Allah' refers only to the God of Islam and not the God of Christianity.

In order to address these questions we need to first consider the linguistic category to which 'Allah' and 'God' belong. Although it is sometimes suggested that these terms are titles akin to 'the President' or 'the Chairperson', it is more plausible to treat them as names, akin to 'Socrates', 'Saturn', and 'Sea Biscuit'. In treating these terms as names we are not presupposing that they refer, for some names are non-referring (or 'empty')—that is, they fail to latch on to an object. Consider, for example, 'Vulcan', a name that was coined in the 19th century for the planet that was hypothesized to be responsible for anomalies in the orbit of Mercury. ('Neptune' had earlier been introduced as the name for a hitherto undetected planet responsible for anomalies in the orbit of Uranus.) 'Vulcan' turned out to be non-referring, for the anomalies in Mercury's orbit were later explained by general relativity rather than the gravitational influence of an undetected planet. Any analysis of religious language should allow that religious terms could turn out to be empty, for that is precisely what atheists claim is the case. In asking what 'God' means we are not presupposing that God exists, but are instead asking a more fundamental question: what must the world be like in order for the term 'God' to refer?

To answer this question we need an account of how names latch on to their objects. In other words, we need a theory of reference. We need an account of how my use of 'Aristotle' (for example) enables me to refer to a particular ancient Greek philosopher. This question would be pressing even if Aristotle was the only person who has been called 'Aristotle', but of course many other people—not to mention dogs, cats, and animals of other kinds—have also had that name.

There are two main accounts of how names refer. Descriptivists hold that a name latches on to an object in virtue of the fact that that object uniquely satisfies the description associated with it. On this view, my use of 'Aristotle' refers to a particular ancient Greek philosopher because he alone satisfies the description that I associate with 'Aristotle', such as 'being the author of the *Nicomachean Ethics*'. If the description that I associate with 'Aristotle' isn't uniquely satisfied—if, for example, the *Nicomachean Ethics* was written by a committee of scholars—then 'Aristotle' would be an empty name in the way that 'Vulcan' is. An alternative account of reference is known as the 'causal view'. Causal theorists hold that names latch on to their referents in virtue of a certain kind of causal chain between the referent and the use of the name. On this view, my use of 'Aristotle' refers to a particular ancient Greek philosopher not because he uniquely satisfies the description that I associate with 'Aristotle', but because there is a causal chain of a certain kind between Aristotle and my use of 'Aristotle'.

Which of these two accounts of reference should be preferred? Although descriptivism might be true of some names (such as terms that are introduced in the context of scientific theories, like 'Neptune' and 'Vulcan'), most philosophers are convinced that ordinary names are best understood in terms of the causal account. An initial baptism takes place—for example, Aristotle's parents announce that he will be called 'Aristotle'—and the name is subsequently passed from speaker to speaker, with the result that you and I can now use 'Aristotle' to refer to Aristotle even though we may not be able to associate 'Aristotle' with any uniquely identifying description. All that we need in order to use 'Aristotle' to refer to Aristotle is a certain kind of causal chain between Aristotle and ourselves.

Our interest, of course, is not with ordinary names such as 'Aristotle', but with religious names such as 'God', 'Allah', and 'Yahweh'. Assuming that 'God' refers, does it do so in virtue of its descriptive content, or in virtue of causal chains of a certain type?

The answer to this question is likely to depend on the kind of religious tradition that is under discussion. Some religious traditions treat God as a theoretical posit, a being whose existence is assumed in order to explain some feature of the world. This approach to theological matters is known as the 'God of the gaps' approach. In traditions of this kind, it is plausible to suppose that 'God' is used descriptively, as a name for that being (if such there be) who uniquely satisfies a certain description. Just as 'Vulcan' was introduced as a name for that planet which was hypothesized to explain the anomalies in Mercury's orbit, so too 'God' might be introduced into a language as a name for that being, whatever its nature, who created the world.

But although some traditions treat God as a theoretical posit, others conceive of God as a being who has been directly encountered in experience and revelation. Certainly this is how the Abrahamic religions regard God. The God of Abraham, Isaac, and Jacob is not regarded as an empty abstraction whose existence is posited in order to account for an otherwise puzzling feature of the world, but as a living being with whom the prophets have come face-to-face. The causal view arguably provides a better account of how religious terms are used within these traditions than the descriptive account does. From this perspective, 'God' ('Yahweh', 'Allah', and so on) refers to whatever supernatural entity it is that has revealed itself to Abraham, Isaac, and Jacob, irrespective of its nature. If no supernatural entity revealed itself to Abraham, Isaac, and Jacob—or if different supernatural entities revealed themselves to Abraham, Isaac, and Jacob—then 'God' would be an empty name.

We are now in a position to address the question of whether religious names ('Allah', 'God', 'Yahweh') could refer to the same being, or whether they refer to different beings (if indeed they refer at all). Let us call the claim that these names refer to the same being the *co-reference thesis*. Assuming that the causal account captures the way in which religious names are understood in these traditions, the truth of the co-reference thesis then depends on the nature of the experiential encounters that are regarded as authoritative in fixing the referent of 'Allah', 'God', and 'Yahweh'. If God's revelation to Abraham, Isaac, and Jacob is taken to be authoritative in determining the referent of these names, then it would follow that Jews, Christians, and Muslims worship the same being (if, that is, they worship any being at all). If, on the other hand, Jews, Christians, and Muslims regard different alleged encounters with the divine as authoritative in fixing the referent of their religious terms, then it would be an open question whether the members of these three faiths worship one and the same being.

In short, although reflection on issues in the philosophy of language can take us some of the way towards answering the questions raised by the ruling of the Malaysian High Court (see the start of this chapter), a full answer to these questions turns on issues that lie beyond the scope of this chapter, for whether different religions might be said to refer to (and worship) the same being depends not only on how the adherents of these religions use the relevant terms, but also on the answers to contested questions about the truth of these religions.

Talking about God

Let us turn now from issues of reference to issues of predication. Religions don't merely refer *to* God, they also make a great many claims *about* God. Some descriptions of God are clearly metaphorical. For example, when the Jewish prophet Jeremiah described Yahweh as his fortress, he clearly meant to be using 'fortress' metaphorically rather than literally. Religious uses of metaphor are interesting, but they are not obviously more problematic than non-religious uses of metaphor, and we will leave them to one side in order to focus on non-metaphorical speech about God. Consider, for example, the claim that God made the world, or that God is good. How should we understand such claims? The question here isn't whether they are true or even reasonable, but rather what they *mean*.

The most straightforward answer to this question is that when predicates are applied to God they mean precisely the same thing that they mean when applied to a human beings or indeed any other mundane object. This view—which is known as the *univocal* (literally: 'one voice') account of religious predication—entails that when God is said to be good or to have made the world, the terms 'good' and 'made' mean just what they mean when Sophie is said to be good or Helen is said to have made the chair.

The univocal view is undoubtedly attractive. For one thing, it can account for the fact that someone who has not previously encountered religious claims knows what is meant when she first hears them. If the terms 'made' and 'good' had entirely novel meanings when applied to God, then one would need to learn these new meanings in order to understand religious language.

But despite its undoubted attractiveness, the univocal faces a number of serious problems. One problem is that a univocal treatment of many predicates is at odds with the standard view of

God as immaterial, disembodied, and atemporal (see Chapters 2 and 3). Consider, for example, the claim that God created the world. Theists typically take God to have created the world *ex nihilo* ('from nothing'), but human creative activity always acts on some pre-existing matter. Consider also the claims that God speaks and deliberates. It is difficult to understand how God could speak on the assumption that God is disembodied; and it is difficult to understand how God could deliberate on the assumption that God is atemporal.

A second problem with the univocal view is that it seems to be at odds with God's transcendence. God, it is often said, is not just another item in the world that might be catalogued alongside goldfish, guitars, and guinea pigs; instead, God is 'Wholly Other'. Many theorists argue that the otherness of God entails that the predicates which are applied to mundane reality cannot be univocally applied to God. Indeed, some theorists hold that God's transcendence entails that it is not possible to speak about God at all. In the words of the French philosopher Jean-Luc Marion, 'a God that could be conceptually comprehended would no longer bear the title "God"'.

One attempt to reconcile the univocal account of religious language with the transcendence of God takes the form of the *via negativa* (the 'negative way'). This position is most closely associated with the writings of the medieval Jewish philosopher Maimonides. In *The Guide for the Perplexed*, Maimonides likened our knowledge of God to the knowledge that a landlubber might have of a ship. Such a person lacks a positive conception of ships, but they do know much about what ships are not. For example, they know that ships are not minerals, plants, or natural objects; that they are neither flat nor spherical; and so on. Maimonides suggests that in the same way that such a person might 'almost arrive' at an understanding of a ship through a process of elimination, so too we can 'almost arrive' at an understanding of God by knowing what God is not.

However, even if proponents of the *via negativa* are able to reconcile the transcendence of God with a univocal account of religious language, in so doing they distance themselves from ordinary religious language, for religious texts are replete with positive descriptions of God's character and activity. In other words, the *via negativa* is best understood not as an account of the way in which language is *actually* used within religious communities, but as an account of how it *should* be used. But if that is so then it fails to provide us with an account of what theists mean when they describe God as (say) the creator of the world.

If the univocal account is unsustainable what might we replace it with? The most influential view of religious language is the *analogical* account. The analogical account can be understood as a compromise between the univocal account on the one hand and the equivocal account on the other, where the equivocal account holds that words mean one thing when applied to human beings and another thing entirely when applied to God (much as 'bank' means one thing when applied to the sides of a river and another when applied to financial institutions). The analogical view treats the religious meaning of terms as *extensions* of their ordinary meanings. As a parallel, consider the term 'leg'. Although 'leg' is primarily used to refer to bodily appendages, we also speak of arguments and ideas—not to mention chairs, tables, and other pieces of furniture—as having legs. These uses are analogical, for we grasp what is meant by an idea 'having legs' by thinking of the function of ordinary legs.

St Thomas Aquinas is perhaps the most famous proponent of the analogical account within the Christian world, but its influence extends well beyond Thomism. That influence is well-deserved, for the analogical account has many of the virtues of the univocal account without suffering from its vices. Because the analogical account holds that the meaning of terms when they are applied to God is related to that which they ordinarily possess, it can explain why people understand religious language when they first encounter it. (By contrast, advocates of the equivocal account have trouble explaining this fact.) The analogical account can also accommodate divine transcendence and the ontological gulf between the Creator and the created. By conceiving of the meaning of religious uses of predicates as extensions of their ordinary meaning, the analogical account can secure the intelligibility of positive speech about God (something denied by the advocates of the *via negativa*) without compromising the radical 'Otherness' of God (as the univocal view threatens to do).

Despite these attractive features, the analogical view also raises many unanswered questions. Perhaps the most critical of these concerns how religious language should be interpreted. It is one thing to know that when predicates are applied to God their meaning involves some kind of analogical extension of that which they ordinarily bear, but how is that extension determined? What ways of extending the ordinary meanings of terms are legitimate and what ways are illegitimate? And—more to the point—how do those who encounter religious language know which ways of extending the ordinary meanings of terms are legitimate and which are illegitimate? We will have a fully comprehensive account of religious language only when these questions have been answered.

Chapter 8
The afterlife

Beyond the grave

In his delightful book, *Sum: Forty Tales from the Afterlives*,
David Eagleman imagines a number of possible afterlives. In one
scenario, we discover that we are enormous, nine-dimensional
beings charged with the maintenance of the cosmos; when we are
exhausted by this work we are reincarnated as humans and
abandon our responsibilities as cosmic caretakers. In another
afterlife scenario, we can choose what kind of creatures we want
to be in the next life. In a third scenario, we recline on leather
couches and inspect banks of televisions, looking for evidence of
our residual impact on the world.

Speculation on the nature of the afterlife is, of course, as old as
recorded history. The Babylonians believed that one's fate
depended on the kind of burial that one had received: those who
had been appropriately buried descended to the underworld,
whereas those who had been deprived of a proper burial were
condemned to wander the Earth as malevolent ghosts. The
ancient Egyptians took the afterlife to involve a paradise called the
Field of Rushes, entry to which involved a perilous journey and an
inquisition before forty-two divine judges. The Aztecs believed
that one's destination in the afterlife was determined by the nature
of one's death: those who died in battle were thought to become

butterflies and hummingbirds; those who died in childbirth were thought to help the sun god move the sun; and those who succumbed to illness or old age were thought to serve the Lord of the Dead in darkness.

Although the doctrine of an afterlife is not found in all religious traditions, where it does occur it is typically central to religious belief and practice. The rituals of Buddhism and Hinduism are designed to improve one's chances of a good rebirth and to hasten liberation from the cycle of birth and rebirth. Members of the Abrahamic religions are exhorted to live their lives mindful of the fact that death is not the end, and that a final judgement awaits us all. It is something of an understatement to say that the question of life after death *matters* to us.

The list of arguments that have been given for thinking that there is an afterlife is long and varied. Some appeal to empirical phenomena, invoking out-of-body experiences and memories—or, perhaps we should say, *putative* memories—of past lives as proof of live after death (and before birth). Others present metaphysical arguments for an afterlife. Plato, for instance, argued that the soul is naturally immortal on the grounds that it has no parts, and what has no parts cannot be subject to decay or dissolution. Still others argue that the demands of justice require an afterlife, for without life beyond the grave there is no prospect that wickedness will be punished and virtue rewarded. The doctrine of reincarnation is also underpinned by a conviction that the world is fundamentally just, for it appeals to prenatal existence to explain why apparently innocent people suffer (they aren't really innocent, but are being punished for evil deeds committed in previous lives) while apparently underserving individuals prosper (they aren't really undeserving, but are being rewarded for their virtuous activity in previous lives).

Despite their philosophical interest, we will leave the various arguments for the existence of an afterlife to one side here.

Instead, we will restrict our attention to a more fundamental question: is the idea of an afterlife intelligible? Are we the sorts of beings that could survive death? And if so, how?

The appeal to souls

One popular view is that we are souls—immaterial substances that are only contingently related to our bodies. This view is known as substance dualism, for it conceives of human beings as composed of two kinds of substances: minds and bodies. If dualism were true then hope for life beyond the grave would certainly be intelligible. If you are a soul then your continued existence does not depend on the continued existence of your body, and you could (in principle, at least) survive its destruction in the way in which a sailor can survive the destruction of her ship.

Although substance dualism has been popular in the history of religious thought, contemporary philosophers of religion—especially those who work within the Christian tradition—tend to express little enthusiasm for it. There are two reasons for this. The first is philosophical. Many theorists are convinced that the best account of our nature identifies us with animals of a certain species (*Homo sapiens*). This view—known as 'animalism'—holds that our identity conditions are purely biological. According to animalism, you came into existence when a certain animal came into existence, and you will go out of existence when that same animal goes out of existence. If we are animals, then the possibility of an afterlife would seem to depend on whether an organism can survive its death. We will return to this issue shortly.

The second—and arguably more influential—reason why few philosophers of religion appeal to dualism in developing an account of the afterlife is theological. Although some religious traditions (such as Zoroastrianism) are explicitly dualistic, dualism is alien to the Abrahamic faiths. The Jewish philosopher Maimonides regarded belief in the resurrection of the body as one of his thirteen Principles of Faith; Christians testify to 'the resurrection of the body and the life everlasting' in reciting the Apostles' Creed; and belief in the Day of Resurrection is central to Islam. From the perspective of the Abrahamic religions, belief in a bodily resurrection isn't an optional 'add-on' to belief in the afterlife—it is what belief in the afterlife amounts to, and for the adherents of these religions questions about the intelligibility of the afterlife are questions about the intelligibility of bodily resurrection.

The reassembly model

Death takes many forms. Some people die peacefully in their beds of natural causes; others are annihilated in explosions; and still others are eaten by cannibals. The doctrine of the resurrection holds that we will all be resurrected, whatever the nature of our death. How could such a thing be possible?

The reassembly model provides one answer to this question. As the name suggests, the reassembly model conceives of resurrection as involving the reassembly in bodily form of the very matter from which one's body was composed at the point of death. Consider a watch that is broken down into its constituents, and then subsequently reassembled. The reconstituted watch is one and the same as that which was disassembled, for it has the same parts and it retains its structural features. Similarly, advocates of the reassembly model hold that Abraham will be resurrected if, at some point after his death, the particles that composed his body are reassembled in the precise form that they took at the point of death.

Although the reassembly model has had many illustrious advocates over the centuries, it has few contemporary proponents. There are good reasons for this, for the objections to the model are many and pressing. One objection concerns the problem of specifying which particles God needs to reassemble in order to reconstitute a person. Different versions of this problem arise depending on the nature of the individual's death. If a person has died of natural causes, then reassembling their particles in the form that they took at the point of death is unlikely to secure their continued existence, for surely such a person would simply die of natural causes again (if indeed they came back to life at all). If a person has been annihilated in an explosion, then the particles that composed their body may no longer exist. If a person has died at the hands of cannibals, then both the cannibal and the cannibal's victim might have a claim to the same particles. St Augustine argued on grounds of priority that it is the cannibal's victim rather than the cannibal who has the legitimate claim on the disputed particles, but what then are we to say about the cannibal's prospects for resurrection?

A further challenge to the reassembly model derives from the very definition of death. Death is typically defined as the *irreversible* cessation of life. Someone whose heart has temporarily stopped beating is not yet dead, for the cessation of their metabolic processes is not irreversible. But if death is the irreversible cessation of life then life after death is a conceptual impossibility, and not even an omnipotent God can do what is conceptually impossible. The organism that God creates from my reassembled atoms might indeed be alive, but its life would not be my life. Instead of securing my post-mortem existence, the reassembly of my atoms would have replaced me with my *doppelgänger*.

Perhaps this objection can be side-stepped by reconceptualizing the nature of death. Rather than thinking of death as involving the irreversible cessation of life, the advocate of the reassembly model might suggest that we should think of death as a state in which in which life has ceased apart from God's miraculous intervention. This account would preserve our ordinary understanding of death, while allowing that it is conceptually possible for an individual to 'come back from the dead', as Lazarus is said to have done in the Gospel of John (Figure 8). The metabolic activity that constituted

8. Duccio di Buoninsegna's 'Raising of Lazarus'.

Lazarus's life was winding down, and this process was irreversible apart from God's miraculous intervention.

Perhaps the most serious objection to the reassembly model is the *gappiness objection*, an objection that is best appreciated by considering a story that is due to the philosopher Peter van Inwagen. Suppose that a group of monks claim to have in their possession a manuscript written by St Augustine. The monks admit that the manuscript was burnt in 457 CE, but they claim that God miraculously recreated it in 458 from the atoms that survived the fire. Van Inwagen argues that the monks' claim could not possibly be true. He allows that God might have collected together precisely the same atoms that composed St Augustine's manuscript, and that God could then have rearranged those atoms in precisely the way that St Augustine's manuscript was arranged, but he denies that this would be a way of reconstituting the original manuscript. Instead, van Inwagen argues, it would simply be a way of creating a perfect duplicate of St Augustine's manuscript. And just as reassembling the atoms that constituted St Augustine's manuscript would not bring it back into existence, so too—van Inwagen argues—reassembling St Augustine's own atoms would not bring him back into existence. Augustine and his *doppelgänger* might be composed of exactly the same atoms, and they might have the same qualitative features, but they would be distinct objects. Why is that?

At the heart of van Inwagen's argument is the assumption that material objects cannot survive periods of non-existence. Unlike political parties, rock bands, or sports teams, material objects cannot be 'existentially gappy'. This assumption can be challenged. Suppose that I disassemble my watch into its components, send those components to different workshops for repair, and then reassemble them once they have been returned to me. Surely this process is consistent with the continued existence of my watch, despite the fact that it no longer exists during the period in which it has been disassembled. (Suppose that my watch is stolen shortly after it is reassembled. It would be odd for my insurer to argue that my insurance claim was void on the grounds that the reassembled watch was merely a *doppelgänger* of the one that I had insured.)

But even if certain kinds of material objects (such as watches) can survive periods of non-existence, it is doubtful whether organisms can. When the identity of an artefact is threatened (for example, when a watch loses a crucial part), it will not take steps to repair itself; organisms, by contrast, are self-repairing entities. The principle of unity for an organism involves the metabolic processes that are responsible for maintaining its borders. It is these processes—processes responsible for what philosophers have referred to as 'immanent causation'—that accounts for the future states of the organism: the infant becomes a child, who in turn becomes a teenager, and so on, each stage leaving its causal imprint on later stages. Organisms cannot survive interruptions to their existence because such interruptions break the chain of immanent causation. The reassembly model invokes God's agency to replace a missing link in this chain of causation, but it is no more possible for God to play this role than it is for God to produce an authentic version of your signature.

Body-snatching and falling elevators

Although van Inwagen rejects the reassembly model, he is by no means opposed to the doctrine of the resurrection; indeed, he himself has proposed an alternative to it: the 'body-snatchers' model. According to the body-snatchers model, immediately prior to the moment of death God replaces a person with a simulacrum of their body. The person themselves is instantaneously transported to another realm (heaven or hell, perhaps), and it is only the simulacrum that is buried, cremated, or eaten by cannibals (as the case may be).

However, it is not clear that the body-snatchers model is much of an improvement on the reassembly model. The most obvious problem with the body-snatchers account is that it represents God as a deceiver. As the philosopher Dean Zimmerman has noted, it would not be unfair to compare the kind of deception implicit in the body-snatching account with that of which God would be guilty if dinosaur bones were fakes designed to fool us into accepting evolutionary theory.

Zimmerman himself has provided a third model of the resurrection: the 'falling elevator' model. According to this view, at the moment of death God gives the atoms in one's body the power to 'bud', with the result that each atom generates an exact duplicate of itself at another location (what Zimmerman calls 'the next world'). These duplicate atoms form a living organism, with the result that one now has two 'bodies': a corpse and a freshly minted body. Zimmerman argues that in this scenario one would survive as the second organism (rather than as one's corpse), because this organism's life would be a continuation of one's own. In some sense, you would have 'jumped' from one body to another. (The 'falling elevator' label is meant to evoke the comic strip image in which a protagonist cheats death by jumping out of a falling elevator at the last minute.)

The falling elevator model avoids the deception that is implicit in the body-snatching account, but it has problems of its own. One might worry that God's involvement in this process—God's role in giving one's atoms the power to bud—is problematic. After all, what is the difference between a scenario in which God gives your atoms the power to bud and a scenario in which God creates duplicates of your atoms and arranges them in the way in which your atoms are currently arranged? For reasons that we have already noted, the latter scenario would not be one in which you are resurrected, but would instead be a scenario in which God creates your *doppelgänger*. Why should we not say the same thing about the former scenario? Moreover, if all of the atoms in one's (newly created) body were arranged as they are precisely at the moment of one's death, then surely those who die of natural causes would be condemned to suffer the same fate again.

Although philosophers have proposed many other accounts of the resurrection, we must leave this topic at this point. As the Apostle Paul noted, the doctrine of the bodily resurrection is indeed a 'mystery'.

Who wants to live forever?

In addition to asking whether life after death is a possible state for creatures like us, we can also ask whether it would be a desirable state for creatures like us. Should we *want* to live forever?

The answer to this question might seem obvious. An eternity of pain, boredom, or loneliness would clearly be unattractive, but wouldn't an eternity in which one was able to enjoy the goods of life be welcome? Death deprives one of a future, and the prospect of a future without limit is surely attractive. One might even argue that the positive value afforded by certain kinds of immortality could offset the badness of any finite life, no matter how bad it was.

But philosophers delight in questioning the obvious, and many have claimed that immortality could not be a good thing for creatures like us. In *Being and Time*, Martin Heidegger (1889–1976) argued that mortality gives meaning to life, for a life without end would be shapeless—it would have no overall structure. In response, one might certainly grant that mortality does impose a certain kind of structure on one's life—as Samuel Johnson once remarked, nothing concentrates the mind like the prospect of being hanged in a fortnight—but there are many other ways in which our lives are shaped. Couldn't one's character and commitments impose structure on even an infinitely extended life? Moreover, it is not entirely clear why a good life must have an overall shape or meaning. Wouldn't it suffice to find some degree of meaning in each and every moment of life? Why must one's life as a whole have a determinate 'shape'?

Another argument for the claim that immortality would not be desirable is due to Bernard Williams (1929–2003). Williams argues that in order to be desirable immortality must meet the following two conditions. First, one must continue to exist as an individual subject of thought and experience. A scenario in which one was absorbed into some form of cosmic consciousness would not secure the kind of immortality that we desire. Second, the state in which one survives must be one that allows the aims that one has in wanting to survive to be realized. Williams invokes Karel Čapek's play *The Makropulos Case* to argue that it is not possible for both of these conditions to be simultaneously satisfied. The eponymous heroine of this play, Elina Makropulos, has reached the age of 342 due to the effects of a life-prolonging elixir, but far from rejoicing in the prospect of immortality she views it with dread. She has become bored with life, and refuses to take the elixir again. Williams argues that Čapek's play captures a deep truth about immortality, and shows that it would be intolerable. 'In those versions of immortality in which I am recognizably myself,' he writes, 'I would eventually have had altogether too much of myself.'

Some have claimed that Williams's argument overlooks the possibility of inexhaustible pleasures—pleasures that one would never tire of no matter how familiar they were. Different people might find different kinds of pleasures inexhaustible, but a list of such pleasures might include those associated with intellectual, aesthetic, and sporting pursuits, not to mention friendship and love. These pleasures do not seem to have any intrinsic limit, and there is no apparent reason why one *must* tire of them. Indeed, theologians and mystics down the ages have conceived of the afterlife as structured around communion with God, an activity that they view as an inexhaustible source of pleasure.

In anticipation of this objection, Williams allows that certain kinds of pleasures might be inexhaustible, but he argues that a life that was focused on such pleasure would not realize one's own immortality. '[I]f one is totally and perpetually absorbed in such an activity, and loses oneself in it...we come back to the problem of satisfying the conditions that it should be me who lives for ever, and that the eternal life should be in prospect of some interest.'

The question, of course, is what precisely it takes for one to survive. Williams assumes that survival requires a certain kind of active self-consciousness, a state in which one is aware of oneself as a subject of experience. It is this form of self-consciousness that is lost when one is absorbed in intellectual, aesthetic, or spiritual pursuits. But it is not at all clear that survival does require self-consciousness of this kind. Consider those moments in which one is captivated by the beauty of nature, and has lost any awareness of oneself. Do we regard such episodes as altogether absent from our autobiographies? I think not. Indeed, many of us regard such episodes as moments in which we are most fully ourselves.

References

Chapter 2: The concept of God

For Descartes on God's power and the necessity of mathematics, see his *Philosophical Letters* (1970, trans. A. Kenny).

For creation as the play of God, see A.L. Herman's 'Indian Theodicy: Samkara and Ramanuja on Brahma Sutra II.1.32–36', *Philosophy East and West* 21, 265–81 (1971).

The passages from the Koran occur at 20:7 and 24:35.

For Boethius on God and time, see his *The Consolations of Philosophy*, James T. Buchanon (ed.), New York, 1957.

The quotation from Grace Jantzen is taken from her 'Time and Timelessness', in Alan Richardson and John Bowden (eds), *A New Dictionary of Christian Theology* (SCM Press, 1983).

For Rachels on the incompatibility between the demands of worship and moral autonomy, see his 'God and Human Attitudes', *Religious Studies* 7, 325–37 (1971).

The quotation from Nietzsche is taken from his book *The AntiChrist*, paragraph 18.

Chapter 3: Arguments for the existence of God

The statement with which this chapter opens is attributed to Russell by Wesley C. Salmon in his 'Religion and Science: A New Look at Hume's *Dialogues*', *Philosophical Studies* 33, 176 (1978).

The quotation from Nozick is taken from his *Philosophical Explanations* (OUP, 1981). The full quotation is as follows:

> To ask 'why is there something rather than nothing?' assumes that nothing(ness) is the natural state that does not need to be explained, while deviations or divergences from nothingness have to be explained...There is, so to speak, a presumption in favor of nothingness. (Nozick 1981, p. 122)

The quotations from Cicero are to be found in Book 2 of his *On the Nature of the Gods* (Harvard University Press, 1933), chapter 38, 97.

J.J.C. Smart's claim that the design argument is guilty of 'psychocentric hubris' can be found in his contribution to *Atheism and Theism* (ed. J.J.C. Smart and John Haldane) (Blackwell, 1996).

Pascal's comments about the psychological impotence of the arguments for God's existence can be found in his Pensées, §190, translated with a revised introduction by A. J. Krailsheimer (Penguin Classics 1966, Revised edition 1995). Copyright © A. J. Krailsheimer, 1966, 1995.

The data regarding religious experiences in the USA are drawn from a Pew survey conducted in 2009. See: <http://www.pewresearch.org/fact-tank/2009/12/29/mystical-experiences/>.

For William Alston on religious experience as perception of God, see his *Perceiving God* (Cornell University Press, 1991). The quoted material appears on p. 24.

Nick Zangwill's objection to the very possibility of religious experiences can be found in his paper 'The Myth of Religious Experience', *Religious Studies* 40, 1–22 (2004).

Michael Martin's objection from religious diversity can be found in his *Atheism: A Philosophical Justification* (Temple University Press, 1990).

The quotation from John Cottingham is taken from his *Philosophy of Religion: Towards a More Human Approach* (Cambridge University Press, 2014), pp. 29–30.

Chapter 4: Divine hiddenness and the nature of faith

The quotation from Nietzsche is from his *Daybreak*, translated by R.J. Hollingdale (Cambridge University Press, 1982), pp. 89–90.

The quotations from J.L. Schellenberg are drawn from his *Divine Hiddenness and Human Reason* (Cornell University Press, 1993), p. 39.

'There is enough light...', see Pascal's *Pensées*, §149, translated by A.J. Krailsheimer (Penguin, 1966).

The Barth quotation can be found in his *Church Dogmatics*, vol. 2, Pt. 1 (T&T Clark, 1957), p. 187.

The quotation from Richard Swinburne is taken from his *The Existence of God* (Clarendon, 2004).

Mark Twain's aphorism on faith appeared in his *Pudd'nhead Wilson's New Calendar* (first published in 1897).

The quotation from Aquinas is from his *Summa Theologica*, vol. 3, II–II, q.1. art.4.

William Clifford's essay 'The Ethics of Belief' was originally published in 1877, and can be found in T. Madigan (ed.), *The Ethics of Belief and other Essays* (Amherst, MA: Prometheus, 1999).

For Peter van Inwagen's discussion of Clifford's Dictum, see his paper, 'It is Wrong, Everywhere, Always, for Anyone, to Believe Anything upon Insufficient Evidence', in J. Jordan and D. Howard-Snyder (eds), *Faith, Freedom and Rationality* (Rowman and Littlefield, 1996), pp. 137–54.

William James' discussion of faith can be found in his essay 'The Will to Believe' (first published in 1896).

The quotations from Søren Kierkegaard are taken from his *Concluding Unscientific Postscript*, translated by D.F. Swenson and W. Lowrie (Princeton University Press, 1941).

Chapter 5: The problem of evil

Epicurus's formulation of the problem of evil is not to be found in his extant writings, but is attributed to him by Lactantius in his *De Ira Dei*, see Lactantius, *The Minor Works*, The Fathers of the Church, Vol. 54, trans. by Sister Mary Francis McDonald (Catholic University of America Press, 1965; reprinted 2010).

The idea that natural evil is required for knowledge of the laws of nature is developed by Richard Swinburne in a number of places, in particular his volume *Providence and the Problem of Evil* (Oxford University Press, 1998).

For John Hick's soul-making theodicy, see his book *Evil and the God of Love* (Palgrave, 1966).

For St Augustine's free will defence, see his *The City of God*.

The passage from J.L. Mackie can be found in his 'Evil and Omnipotence', *Mind* 64, 200–12 (1955). The argument can also be found in his *The Miracle of Theism* (Oxford University Press, 1982).

For Alvin Plantinga's free will defence, see his *God, Freedom and Evil* (Eerdmans, 1974).

For the notion of a horrendous evil, see Marilyn McCord Adams's *Horrendous Evil and the Goodness of God* (Cornell University Press, 1999).

Hans Küng's description of the problem of evil as 'the rock of atheism' can be found in his *On Being a Christian* (Doubleday, 1976).

Chapter 6: The roots of religious belief

The quotation from Diodorus Siculus is taken from lib.iii.47 (cited in Hume's *Natural History of Religion*).

Hume's reference to religion as arises chiefly from anxious fear is to be found in his *Natural History of Religion*.

The quote from Freud is to be found in his *The Future of an Illusion* (Hogarth Press, 1964), p. 25.

The quotation from Marx can be found in the introduction to his *Critique of Hegel's Philosophy of Right*, trans. A. Jolin and J. O'Malley (Cambridge University Press, 1970).

On the existence of a hypersensitive agency detection device, see Stewart Guthrie's *Faces in the Clouds: A New Theory of Religion* (Oxford University Press, 1993).

For the experiments by Heider and Simmel on the perception of agency, see their 'An Experimental Study of Apparent Behavior', *American Journal of Psychology* 57(2), 243–59 (1944).

For Paul Bloom on intuitive dualism and religion, see his 'Religion is Natural', *Developmental Science* 10(1), 147–51 (2007); and 'Is God an Accident?' *The Atlantic* December (2005).

For Deborah Kelemen on teleological explanation in preschoolers, see her 'The Scope of Teleological Thinking in Preschool Children', *Cognition* 70, 241–72 (1999).

On religion as ensuring norm compliance, see Dominic Johnson and Oliver Kruger, 'The Good of Wrath: Supernatural Punishment and the Evolution of Cooperation', *Political Theology* 5: 159–76

(2004); Azim Shariff and Ara Norenzayan, 'God is Watching
You', *Psychological Science* 18(9), 803–9 (2007); and Dominic
Johnson and Jesse Bering, 'Hand of God, Mind of Man', in
J. Schloss and M. Murray (eds), *The Believing Primate: Scientific,
Philosophical, and Theological Reflections on the Origin of
Religion* (Oxford University Press, 2010).

For Peter Kail on vindicatory, destabilizing, and neutral paths to belief,
see his 'Understanding Hume's *Natural History of Religion*', *The
Philosophical Quarterly* 57, 190–211 (2007).

The line of Tim Mawson's is taken from his excellent paper 'The
Cognitive Science of Religion and the Rationality of Classical
Theism', in R. Trigg and J. Barrett (eds), *The Roots of Religion*
(Ashgate, 2014).

Chapter 7: Speaking of God

The quotation from D.Z. Phillips is taken from his book *Religion
without Explanation* (Basil Blackwell, 1976), p. 181.

For Janet Soskice's description of verificationism as 'dissolving in its
own acids', see her article 'Religious Language', in C. Taliaferro,
P. Draper, and P.L. Quinn (eds), *A Companion to Philosophy of
Religion* (Blackwell, 2010).

The quotation from Roger Trigg is taken from his book *Rationality
and Religion* (Blackwell, 1998), p. 49.

For the quotation from Jean-Luc Marion, see his 'In the Name:
How to Avoid Speaking of "Negative Theology"', In J.D. Caputo
and M.J. Scanlon (eds), *God, the Gift, and Postmodernism*
(Bloomington, 1999), p. 34.

Chapter 8: The afterlife

For St Augustine on cannibalism and the afterlife, see his *The
Enchiridion on Faith, Hope and Love* (book 88); see also his *City
of God*, 22.20.

For Peter van Inwagen's body-snatching account of resurrection, see
his 'The Possibility of Resurrection', *International Journal of
Philosophy of Religion* 9, 114–21 (1978); reprinted in his *The
Possibility of Resurrection and Other Essays in Christian
Apologetics* (Westview, 1998).

For Dean Zimmerman's falling elevator model of resurrection, see his
'The Compatibility of Materialism and Survival: The "Falling

Elevator" Model', *Faith and Philosophy* 16, 194–212 (1999); reprinted in E. Stump and M. Murray (eds), *Philosophy of Religion: The Big Questions* (Blackwell, 1999), pp. 379–86.

For Bernard Williams's argument against the desirability of immortality, see his 'The Makropoulos Case: Reflections on the Tedium of Mortality', reprinted in his *Problems of the Self* (Cambridge University Press, 1973), pp. 82–100.

Further reading

Chapter 1: What is the philosophy of religion?

Philosophers of religion operate with very different conceptions of the appropriate relationship between theology and the philosophy of religion. For one perspective on this issue, see Eleonore Stump's 'Athens and Jerusalem: The Relationship of Philosophy and Theology', *Journal of Analytic Theology* 1 (2013).

Chapter 2: The concept of God

For two recent non-theistic accounts of the divine, see Mark Johnston's *Saving God: Religion after Idolatry* (Princeton University Press, 2009); and Michael P. Levine's *Pantheism: A Non-Theistic Concept of Deity* (Routledge, 2014).

Detailed discussion of the issues raised in this chapter can be found in Richard Gale's *On the Nature and Existence of God* (Cambridge University Press, 1991); and Richard Swinburne's *The Coherence of Theism* (Oxford University Press, 1993). Among the many examples of the Anselmian or 'Perfect Being' approach to the philosophy of religion are Brian Leftow's *God and Necessity* (Oxford University Press, 2012); and Thomas V. Morris's *Anselmian Explorations: Essays in Philosophical Theology* (University of Notre Dame Press, 1987).

Further discussion of the divine attributes can be found in Joshua Hoffman and Gary S. Rosenkrantz's *The Divine Attributes* (Blackwell, 2002). For more on the question of whether God could have created abstract objects, see Peter van Inwagen's 'God and Other Uncreated Things', in K. Timpe (ed.), *Metaphysics and*

God: Essays in Honor of Eleonore Stump (Routledge, 2009); and
  Thomas V. Morris and Christopher Menzel's 'Absolute Creation',
  American Philosophical Quarterly 23, 53–362 (1986).
For further discussion of the Euthyphro dilemma, see Philip L. Quinn's
  Divine Commands and Moral Requirements (Oxford: Clarendon
  Press, 1978); T.J. Mawson's 'God's Creation of Morality', Religious
  Studies 38, 1–25 (2002); and Robert M. Adams's Finite and
  Infinite Goods (Oxford University Press, 1999).
A classic discussion of the alleged incompatibility between God's
  omniscience and human free will can be found in Nelson Pike's
  paper 'Divine Omniscience and Voluntary Action', The Philosophical
  Review 74, 27–46 (1965). For further discussions of this topic, see
  J. M. Fischer (ed.) God, Foreknowledge, and Freedom (Stanford
  University Press, 1989); and Linda Zagzebski's The Dilemma of
  Freedom and Foreknowledge (Oxford University Press, 1991).
A defence of the atemporal conception of God can be found in
  Brian Leftow's Time and Eternity (Cornell University Press,
  1991). For further discussions of the relationship between God
  and time, see Richard Swinburne's 'God and Time', in E. Stump
  (ed.), Reasoned Faith (Cornell University Press, 1993); Nicholas
  Wolterstorff's 'God Everlasting', in S. Cahn and D. Shatz (eds),
  Contemporary Philosophy of Religion (Oxford University Press,
  1982); William Lane Craig's God, Time and Eternity (Kluwer,
  2001); and A.G. Padgett's God, Eternity and the Nature of Time
  (Macmillan, 1992).
For a response to Rachels' argument alleging the existence of an
  incompatibility between worship and moral autonomy, see Philip
  L. Quinn's 'Religious Obedience and Moral Autonomy', Religious
  Studies 11, 265–81 (1975).

Chapter 3: Arguments for the existence of God

The two classic treatments of arguments for God's existence are
  Richard Swinburne's The Existence of God (Clarendon Press, 1991),
  which defends the arguments; and J.L. Mackie's The Miracle of
  Theism (Oxford University Press, 1982), which rejects them. Also
  excellent are T.J. Mawson's Belief in God (Oxford University Press,
  2005); and Graham Oppy's Arguing about Gods (Cambridge
  University Press, 2006).
On the cosmological argument in particular, see Derek Parfit's
  'Why Anything? Why This?' London Review of Books 20, 24–7

(22 January 1998). *The Puzzle of Existence: Why is there Something Rather than Nothing?* (Routledge, 2013), edited by Tyron Goldschmidt, contains a number of essays that address the volume's titular question. For an engaging entry into the puzzles of existence, see Jim Holt's *Why Does the World Exist?* (Norton and Co, 2012). A recent and sophisticated defence of the cosmological argument can be found in Timothy O'Connor's *Theism and Ultimate Explanation: The Necessary Shape of Contingency* (Blackwell, 2008).

God and Design: The Teleological Argument and Modern Science (Routledge, 2003), edited by Neil Manson, is a comprehensive collection of papers on the design argument, and the editor's introduction to the volume provides an excellent entry point into the debate. Also useful is Benjamin Jantzen's *An Introduction to Design Arguments* (Cambridge University Press, 2014); and Elliot Sober's (challenging) 'The Design Argument', in the *Blackwell Guide to Philosophy of Religion* (Blackwell, 2005). For the multiverse reply to the fine-tuning argument, see John Leslie's *Universes* (Routledge, 1989); Rodney Holder's *God, the Multiverse, and Everything: Modern Cosmology and the Argument* from Design (Ashgate, 2004); and a number of the essays in *God and Design*. For a fascinating discussion of the science behind the fine-tuning argument, see Martin Rees's *Just Six Numbers: The Deep Forces that Shape the Universe* (Basic Books, 2001).

Caroline Davis's *The Evidential Force of Religious Experience* (Oxford University Press, 1989); and Wayne Proudfoot's *Religious Experience* (University of California Press, 1985) provide good entry points into the argument from religious experience. William James's *The Varieties of Religious Experience* (Longmans Green and Co., 1902) and Evelyn Underhill's *Mysticism: A Study in the Nature and Development of Man's Spiritual Consciousness* (Methuen, 1911) remain classic discussions of religious experience itself.

Chapter 4: Divine hiddenness and the nature of faith

Excellent presentations of J.L. Schellenberg's hiddenness objection to theistic belief can be found in his *Divine Hiddenness and Human Reason* (Cornell University Press, 1993) and *The Hiddenness Argument: Philosophy's New Challenge to Belief in God* (Oxford University Press, 2015). *Divine Hiddenness: New Essays* (Cambridge University Press, 2002), edited by Daniel

Howard-Snyder and Paul K. Moser, contains an engaging set of discussions of the hiddenness argument. Further discussions of divine hiddenness can be found in Robert McKim's 'The Hiddenness of God', *Religious Studies* 26, 141–61 (1990) and Michael J. Murray and David E. Taylor's entry on 'Hiddenness' in *The Routledge Companion to Philosophy of Religion*, edited by Chad Meister and Paul Copan (Routledge, 2012).

Robert Merrihew Adam's essay 'The Virtue of Faith', in his *The Virtue of Faith and Other Essays in Philosophical Theology* (Oxford University Press, 1987), is an important discussion of its titular subject. Adams also provides an illuminating discussion of Kierkegaard's attitudes to religious faith in his paper 'Kierkegaard's Arguments Against Objective Reasoning in Religion,' in S.M. Cahn and D. Shatz (eds), *Contemporary Philosophy of Religion* (Oxford University Press, 1982). Among the many excellent discussions of faith in recent years are John Bishop's *Believing by* Faith (Clarendon Press, 2007); Daniel Howard-Snyder's 'Propositional Faith: What it is and What it is Not', *American Philosophical Quarterly* 50, 357–72 (2013); Jonathan Kvanvig's 'Affective Theism and People of Faith', in Howard Wettstein (ed.), *Midwest Studies in Philosophy* 37, 109–28 (2013); and Terence Penelhum's *Reason and Religious Faith* (Westview Press, 1995). *Religious Faith and Intellectual Virtue* (Oxford University Press, 2014), edited by Laura Frances Callahan and Timothy O'Connor, contains an excellent collection of essays on that very topic.

Chapter 5: The problem of evil

Further discussion of the problem of evil can be found in Peter van Inwagen's *The Problem of Evil* (Oxford University Press, 2006); and Eleonore Stump's *Wandering in Darkness: Narrative and the Problem of Suffering* (Oxford University Press, 2010).

The notion of a horrendous evil was introduced by Marilyn McCord Adams, and is discussed at length in her book *Horrendous Evil and the Goodness of God* (Cornell University Press, 1999). See also Nicholas Wolterstorff's 'The Silence of the God Who Speaks', in *Divine Hiddenness: New Essays* (Cambridge University Press, 2002), edited by Daniel Howard-Snyder and Paul K. Moser.

An important source for the sceptical response to the problem of evil is Stephen J. Wykstra's 'The Humean Obstacle to Evidential Arguments from Suffering: On Avoiding the Evils of

"Appearance"', reprinted in M.M. Adams and R.M. Adams (eds), *The Problem of Evil* (Oxford University Press, 1990). Further discussion of sceptical theism can be found in many of the contributions to Daniel Howard-Snyder's (ed.), *The Evidential Argument from Evil* (Indiana University Press, 2008), in particular William P. Alston's 'The Inductive Argument from Evil and the Human Cognitive Condition'; and Peter van Inwagen's 'The Problem of Evil, the Problem of Air, and the Problem of Silence'.

Chapter 6: The roots of religious belief

A huge amount has been written on the cognitive science of religion in recent years. The following provide good entry points into the field: Scott Attran's *In Gods We Trust: The Evolutionary Landscape of Religion* (Oxford University Press, 2002); Justin Barrett's *Why Would Anyone Believe in God?* (2004); Pascal Boyer's *Religion Explained: The Evolutionary Origins of Religious Thought* (Basic Books, 2001); Daniel Dennett's *Breaking the Spell* (Viking, 2006); Stewart Guthrie's *Faces in the Clouds: A New Theory of Religion* (Oxford University Press, 1993); and Iikka Pyysiäinen's *Supernatural Agents: Why We Believe in Souls, Gods, and Buddhas* (Oxford University Press, 2009).

There have also been a number of thoughtful discussions of the implications of this work for the epistemic status of religious belief. Good to places to begin include: *The Believing Primate: Scientific, Philosophical, and Theological Reflections on the Origin of Religion*, edited by Jeffrey Schloss and Michael Murray (Oxford University Press, 2010); *A New Science of Religion*, edited by Gregory Dawes and James Maclaurin (Routledge, 2013); and *A Natural History of Natural Theology* (MIT Press, 2015), by Helen De Cruz and J. De Smedt.

Chapter 7: Speaking of God

A detailed presentation of D.Z. Phillips's 'Wittgensteinian' treatment of religious language can be found in his books *Faith and Philosophical Enquiry* (Routledge & Kegan Paul, 1970) and *Religion without Explanation* (Basil Blackwell, 1976). For more on the question of how reference of 'God' might be determined, see the contributions to *Referring to God*, edited by Paul Helm

(Palgrave, 2000). For further discussion of religious predication and religious language more generally, see William Alston's *Divine Nature and Human Language* (Cornell University Press, 1989); Michael Scott's *Religious Language* Palgrave, 2013); Janet Martin Soskice's *Metaphor and Religious Language* (Oxford University Press, 1985); and Roger White's *Talking About God* (Ashgate, 2010).

Chapter 8: The afterlife

For soul-based accounts of post-mortem existence, see Terence Penelhum's *Survival and Disembodied Existence* (Routledge, 1970); and Richard Swinburne's *The Resurrection of God Incarnate* (Clarendon, 2003).

Critical discussion of the body-snatchers and falling elevator models can be found in Eric Olson's 'Immanent Causation and Life after Death', in *Personal Identity and Resurrection*, edited by G. Gasser (Ashgate, 2010), pp. 51–66; David Hershenov's 'Van Inwagen, Zimmerman, and the Materialist Conception of Resurrection', *Religious Studies* 38, 451–69 (2002); and Lynne Rudder Baker's 'Death and the Afterlife', in William Wainwright (ed.), *The Oxford Handbook of Philosophy of Religion* (Oxford University Press, 2007). Alternative accounts of the afterlife can be found in Rudder Baker's paper 'Persons and the Metaphysics of Resurrection', *Religious Studies* 43, 333–48 (2007); and Mark Johnston's *Surviving Death* (Princeton University Press, 2010).

Further reflections on the desirability of immortality can be found in Timothy Chappell's 'Infinity Goes Up on Trial: Must Immortality be Meaningless?', *European Journal of Philosophy* 17, 30–44 (2009); John Martin Fisher's 'Why Immortality is Not so Bad', *International Journal of Philosophical Studies* 2, 257–70 (1993); and Adrian Moore's 'Williams, Nietzsche, and the Meaninglessness of Immortality', *Mind* 115, 311–30 (2006).

Publisher's acknowledgements

We are grateful for permission to include the following copyright material in this book.

Excerpt from Summa Theologica by St. Thomas Aquinas, translated by Fathers of the English Dominican Province, © 1948 by Benzinger Bros., New York, NY. Used with the permission of the publisher, Christian Classics™, an imprint of Ave Maria Press®, Inc., Notre Dame, Indiana 46556, www.avemariapress.com.

Extracts from Kierkegaard, copyright (2006), from *Historical introduction to philosophy* edited by Albert B. Hakim. Reproduced by permission of Taylor and Francis Group, LLC, a division of Informa plc.

The publisher and author have made every effort to trace and contact all copyright holders before publication. If notified, the publisher will be pleased to rectify any errors or omissions at the earliest opportunity.

Index

Index

Agnosticism
A Very Short Introduction
Robin Le Poidevin

What is agnosticism? Is it just the 'don't know' position on God, or is there more to it than this? Is it a belief, or merely the absence of belief? Who were the first to call themselves 'agnostics'? These are just some of the questions that Robin Le Poidevin considers in this *Very Short Introduction*. He sets the philosophical case for agnosticism and explores it as a historical and cultural phenomenon. What emerges is a much more sophisticated, and much more interesting, attitude than a simple failure to either commit to, or reject, religious belief. Le Poidevin challenges some preconceptions and assumptions among both believers and non-atheists, and invites the reader to rethink their own position on the issues.

EXISTENTIALISM
A Very Short Introduction
Thomas Flynn

Existentialism was one of the leading philosophical movements of the twentieth century. Focusing on its seven leading figures, Sartre, Nietzsche, Heidegger, Kierkegaard, de Beauvoir, Merleau-Ponty and Camus, this *Very Short Introduction* provides a clear account of the key themes of the movement which emphasized individuality, free will, and personal responsibility in the modern world. Drawing in the movement's varied relationships with the arts, humanism, and politics, this book clarifies the philosophy and original meaning of 'existentialism' - which has tended to be obscured by misappropriation. Placing it in its historical context, Thomas Flynn also highlights how existentialism is still relevant to us today.

www.oup.com/vsi

GERMAN
PHILOSOPHY
A Very Short Introduction
Andrew Bowie

German Philosophy: A Very Short Introduction discusses the idea that German philosophy forms one of the most revealing responses to the problems of 'modernity'. The rise of the modern natural sciences and the related decline of religion raises a series of questions, which recur throughout German philosophy, concerning the relationships between knowledge and faith, reason and emotion, and scientific, ethical, and artistic ways of seeing the world. There are also many significant philosophers who are generally neglected in most existing English-language treatments of German philosophy, which tend to concentrate on the canonical figures. This *Very Short Introduction* will include reference to these thinkers and suggests how they can be used to question more familiar German philosophical thought.

CATHOLICISM
A Very Short Introduction
Gerald O'Collins

Despite a long history of external threats and internal strife, the
Roman Catholic Church and the broader reality of Catholicism
remain a vast and valuable presence into the third millennium of
world history. What are the origins of the Catholic Church? How
has Catholicism changed and adapted to such vast and diverse
cultural influences over the centuries? What great challenges
does the Catholic Church now face in the twenty-first century,
both within its own life and in its relation to others around the
world? In this Very Short Introduction, Gerald O'Collins draws on
the best current scholarship available to answer these questions
and to present, in clear and accessible language, a fresh
introduction to the largest and oldest institution in the world.

www.oup.com/vsi

HUMANISM
A Very Short Introduction
Stephen Law

Religion is currently gaining a much higher profile. The number of faith schools is increasingly, and religious points of view are being aired more frequently in the media. As religion's profile rises, those who reject religion, including humanists, often find themselves misunderstood, and occasionally misrepresented. Stephen Law explores how humanism uses science and reason to make sense of the world, looking at how it encourages individual moral responsibility and shows that life can have meaning without religion. Challenging some of the common misconceptions, he seeks to dispute the claims that atheism and humanism are 'faith positions' and that without God there can be no morality and our lives are left without purpose.

www.oup.com/vsi